KT-230-326

FLOWER ARRANGING

Judith Blacklock

TEACH YOURSELF BOOKS

Acknowledgements

With grateful thanks to the author's mother, Joan Ward, and to the research institute at the Aalsmeer Flower Auction, Holland

Long-renowned as the authoritative source for self-guided learning – with more than 3 million copies sold worldwide – the *Teach Yourself* series includes over 200 titles in the fields of languages, crafts, hobbies, sports, and other leisure activities.

British Library Cataloguing in Publication Data
Blacklock, Judith
   Teach yourself flower arranging
   I. Title
   745.92

Library of Congress Catalog Card Number: 92-80884

First published in UK 1992 by Hodder Headline Plc, 338 Euston Road, London NW1 3BH

First published in US 1992 by NTC Publishing Group,
An Imprint of NTC/Contemporary Publishing Company
4255 West Touhy Avenue, Lincolnwood (Chicago), Illinois 60646 – 1975 U.S.A.

The 'Teach Yourself' name and logo are registered trade marks of Hodder & Stoughton in the UK.

Copyright © 1992 Judith Blacklock

In UK: All rights reserved. No part of this publication may be reproduced or transmitted in any form or by any means, electronic or mechanical, including photocopy, recording, or any information storage and retrieval system, without permission in writing from the publisher or under licence from the Copyright Licensing Agency Limited. Further details of such licences (for reprographic reproduction) may be obtained from the Copyright Licensing Agency Limited, of 90 Tottenham Court Road, London W1P 9HE.

In US: All rights reserved. No part of this book may be reproduced, stored in a retrieval system, or transmitted in any form, or by any means, electronic, mechanical, photocopying, or otherwise, without prior permission of NTC/Contemporary Publishing Comapny.

Photographs by Roddy Paine
Illustrations by Kate Simunek
Flowers supplied by Broadway Florists

Photoset by Intype, London.
Printed in Great Britain by Cox & Wyman Ltd, Reading, Berkshire.

Impression number   13 12 11 10 9 8 7
Year   1999 1998 1997

—————— CONTENTS ——————

About the author

Judith Blacklock is an experienced teacher of flower arranging, including the City and Guilds qualification. She currently runs the Study Plan Flower Arranging programme at Richmond Adult and Community College, and is an area judge for The National Association of Flower Arrangement Societies (NAFAS).

—— INTRODUCTION ——

Any vase or bowl of flowers adds colour and beauty to life, so why arrange flowers? Flower arranging is not just placing stems at certain angles. To learn to arrange flowers is to gain a knowledge and understanding of plant material which will enable you to create with minimum outlay designs that will show up flowers and foliage to greater advantage. They will last longer because you will know what to look for when choosing flowers and how to prepare them.

You may not think of yourself as a creative person but if you learn the rules and follow the instructions in this book you will be able to arrange flowers successfully. Once confident of being able to make basic designs you will surprise yourself by finding a latent creativity you never dreamt existed. If you then go on to break the rules, you will do it with style.

You will grow to have a greater awareness of nature around you. A walk will not be merely a question of exercise. It will become a journey of discovery. You will appreciate the many treasures nature gives without charge. Unconsciously you will start to understand the elements and principles of design. All the arts allied to flower arranging, such as garden and interior design, painting and sculpture, will become more comprehensible and therefore more interesting.

And if this were not enough, arranging flowers is totally absorbing. It is easy to lose yourself and to experience total relaxation. Cares, problems and worries will all be forgotten. Flower arranging is therapeutic.

Worthwhile friendships develop through the medium of flowers. Start with this book, join a flower club where all the bits and pieces for successful arranging can be purchased easily and cheaply and your world will take on an exciting new dimension.

Shrubs, houseplants and flowers often have a common name as well as a botanical name. Where the common name is well known this is the name that is used. The botanical name is only given when it will help you with identification and not confuse you.

1
FLOWERS
— AND FOLIAGE AND HOW —
TO CARE FOR THEM

The key to successful flower arranging is to get the right combination of material together before you start. If the choice is right and you know how to make your plant material last, you will be able to create successful designs, with ease and at little expense, which will last for two weeks or more.

There are two types of plant material which are usually needed to give a cohesive design: *flowers* and *foliage*. An arrangement can be made without flowers but a successful design without foliage is rare. Look at the fifth colour photograph in the plate section and compare it with the drawing below which is the same design without foliage. See how strange and empty it appears.

Everyone has access to some foliage and this chapter will explain how easily it can be found. If you need justification for cutting from a friend's or neighbour's garden, remember that selected pruning not only encourages growth but also improves the shape.

All plant material, whether foliage or flowers, can be divided into one of four shapes:

- Line (foliage or flowers)
- Focal (usually flowers)
- Concealer (usually foliage)
- Filler (foliage or flowers)

Understanding these four different shapes is far more useful than learning all the Latin and Greek names. Each shape has a special purpose in flower arranging. When combined together as shown in this book you will discover just how easy flower arranging can be.

—— Shapes of material required ——

Line material

Line material is used to create the shape or form of the design: its *skeleton*. This skeleton sets the limits to the arrangement. Other material will reinforce but will not go beyond these limits. Line material looks as it sounds. A blade of grass forms a line. A branch of blossom forms a line – though not so straight. Many stems of foliage can be pruned to form line material.

Line foliage is often reinforced by line flowers such as larkspur, gladioli or Canterbury bells which can be positioned almost to the boundaries of the design created by the line foliage.

Line material can be curved or straight. Curved material is essential for shapes such as the upward and downward crescents. It is frequently found on shrubs where the underpart strives for sunlight and curves upwards round the upper parts of the shrub. Rosemary, winter jasmine and broom are good examples.

Long and supple stems can be eased into curves by stroking slowly and gently with warm hands. Broom, sprays of ivy and dogwood respond well to this treatment.

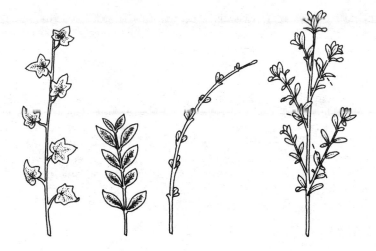

Line material: ivy, privet, pussy willow and escallonia

Concealer material

Concealer material consists of unfussy 'roundish' leaves. It has three important functions.

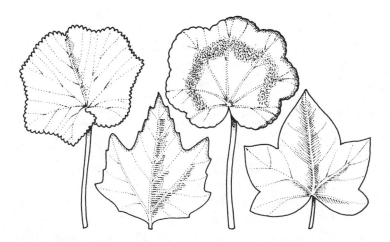

Concealer material: *Alchemilla mollis*, Virginia creeper, geranium, ivy

- It is a means of covering foam and the harsh rim of the container without the arrangement becoming fussy and over-crowded. Once it is in place the arranger often gives a sigh of relief. He or she will have enough material to fill the design after all.
- Concealer material, by virtue of its flat, calm, 'roundish' surfaces acts as a foil to the beauty of other, more showy material. It gives a quiet area on which the eye can rest.
- Its strong plain shape gives visual weight low down in the design where it is needed for good balance. Ivy and geranium leaves are good examples, but leaves such as laurel and magnolia are too *ovate* (long and oval) to work except in large arrangements. Concealer material is usually foliage rather than flowers.

Focal material

Focal material is usually flowers rather than foliage. The flowers have a 'roundish' shape and they are used low in the arrangement but away from the limits established by the line material. They are placed in the central area above the rim of the container. Hydrangeas, peonies, full roses, gerberas, poppies, marigolds, daisies, sweet williams and chrysanthemums are good examples of focal material. Foliage is sometimes used, for example a rosette of London pride.

Focal flowers: hydrangea, daisy chrysanthemum, rose

Focal material is placed in the central area because a symmetrical enclosed shape is the most dominant and eye-catching shape. It is eye-catching because any such shape has an inward directional movement to a central point where the eye is held in momentary suspense from the quiet movement of the composition. The eye does not linger on a line because the eye moves along and away.

Look at a painting or advertisement and see how your eye is drawn first to a 'roundish' shape before moving on to look at the detail of the whole. Your eye will then return to this more dominant shape. You have therefore spent longer looking at the painting or advert thanks to this form. Think also of the pull of open eyes, oranges in a bowl, headlights, dice and traffic lights.

In flower arranging the eye needs a main attraction. This feature, or *focal area*, should be low down and central, but not at the bottom limits of the arrangement. There are three reasons for this:

- A low central area provides the best position for the eye to travel around all the other details of the design before returning to the feature giving the strongest pull.
- Dominant heavier shapes need to be low in a design for good visual balance.
- The low central area is where the stems of line material meet. Focal flowers prevent a 'stemmy' look and unify the converging line material.

N.B. Some books use the word 'point' to denote focal material.

Filler material

Filler material is used to complete the arrangement. It should cover any visible remaining foam or pinholder and give further interest to the design. Filler material is often shrubby and compact, with leaves giving interest down the stem. It is plant material which does not fall into any of the other three categories.

Examples are holly, pittosporum, skimmia, hebe and euonymus (see the next page). Flowers as fillers could be freesia, alstroemeria, cow parsley, asters or lady's mantle (*Alchemilla mollis*) giving colour, scent or a change of texture or form.

The garden is obviously a good source of plant material and there is more information about suitable plants for a flower arranger's garden

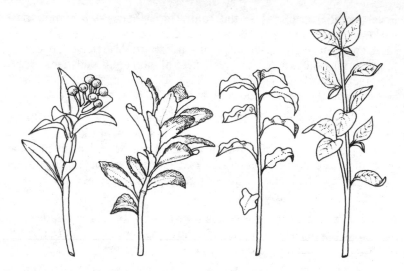

Filler material: skimmia, euonymus, pittosporum, *Viburnum tinus*

later on in this book. It is not essential, however, to have a garden in order to arrange flowers. All the basic arrangements in the following chapters (which can with more experience be adapted for Buckingham Palace itself) could be made from the materials in the section below, most of which are accessible to all.

Foliage

Ivy

The long sprays can be used as straight or curved line material and individual leaves as concealers. The dark green common ivy is a wonderful foil to other more showy material. Ivy is easy to cultivate. It is evergreen, available twelve months of the year and grows in sun or shade. When cut it lasts for weeks if properly treated. It can be grown in tubs, on a patio or outside the front door, or in window boxes, hanging baskets and as a house plant. However, if all these methods of cultivation are not possible then you can gather ivy from hedgerows, river banks or scrubland. Picking from the wild is usually permissible if you are discriminating and only take plant material that is plentiful.

Other good ivies are the neat bright yellow variegated 'Goldheart', 'Cristata' with a fascinating frilly leaf edge, and 'Sulphur Heart' for those planning large arrangements. There are many more.

Geraniums

Although known universally as geraniums, they should strictly speaking be called zonal pelargoniums. Their leaves are excellent concealers and the flowers are a wonderful bonus as focal or filler material.

The leaves last well in a pinholder or foam. Like the ivy they grow well in tubs, window boxes and hanging baskets and need little watering to survive. They bloom in the garden until the first severe frosts. If lifted before this time and taken inside they can be used as a houseplant. They can be grouped with other houseplants and used for their leaves which continue to grow during the winter months. There are many delightful varieties to choose for their scent and leaf colour. Many see the 'legginess' of the older plants to be a disadvantage. Flower arrangers, however, see it as a wonderful opportunity to prune and use!

Privet

Privet is a much under-estimated plant. It gives excellent line material and can be used as a filler in larger arrangements. Privet is evergreen except in the most severe of winters. It is easy to grow in any part of the country and is tolerant of sun, shade and pollution. It can be grown as part of a hedge or as a specimen plant with glorious swaying branches which can create quite a feature.

Built-up areas abound with privet bushes which need constant trimming. Friends and neighbours will rarely say no to your request for a few clippings. Many of our native hedgerows contain privet. In summer small clusters of fragrant white flowers appear. Black berries replace the flowers in the autumn. They are long-lasting and most attractive. The leaves can be stripped from the stem to give them more attention. The yellow variegated privet *Ligustrum ovalifolium* 'Aureo-marginatum' gives sunshine to any arrangement.

Viburnum tinus *(Common name Laurustinus)*

Viburnum tinus is an evergreen shrub which may be unknown to you by name. However, viburnum is an indispensable filler. Large branches provide line material, shorter pieces filler. It is a great joy to all flower arrangers. There are many viburnums but the *Viburnum tinus* is readily available from garden centres, is easy to grow in sun or shade and is inexpensive to purchase. It produces lustrous black berries from September to April and has tight pink buds. At the tight bud stage the flowers do not last if they are cut. However, from January to April the buds develop into creamy flowers, with a pink back to the petals, and these do last well when cut. The subtlety of its colour means viburnum can be added to all arrangements and makes flower arranging inexpensive at a time when flowers are costly to buy. Varieties 'Lucidum' and 'French White' grow more quickly than the others – all the more to cut! The variety 'Gwellian' seems to produce most berries.

Tolmeia (Pig-a-back plant)

This is an extremely easy-going evergreen house plant providing concealer leaves which last well once cut. It can be placed anywhere in the house but is particularly tolerant of cold conditions. It can also be grown outdoors as ground cover.

The leaves are mid-green. Young leaves grow on top of mature leaves for charming effect. These can be easily removed if you wish. Taking cuttings from this plant is easy. Short stems are cut from the mother plant and placed in water. Several weeks later many will have roots and can be placed in potting compost which can be purchased from garden nurseries.

Rosemary

Rosemary provides curved or straight line material. This fragrant evergreen shrub grows easily in tubs, windowboxes and plant pots. It can be grown indoors as a house plant but does need to be grown in a sunny aspect. The delicate blue flowers in spring are a delightful bonus.

Skimmia

Skimmia is an evergreen filler. It has shiny ovate leaves encircling creamy pink flowers in March/April which are followed by glossy red berries which persist all winter. To bear berries, some varieties of skimmia need separate male and female plants, closely planted, but the *Skimmia reevesiana* has the ability to produce berries without a partner. It grows easily, is troublefree in shade or sun, and can be grown from a cutting quite successfully. However, it grows best in gardens which are not too chalky, so if there is a lot of lime in your soil add some peat. Alternatively choose *Skimmia japonica*, but then you will need two plants.

Flowering currant

Flowering currant or *Ribes*, although often ignored or even dug up, is an excellent source of line and concealer material. The roundish leaves turn glorious shades of red and orange and are amongst the last leaves to fall in late autumn, early winter. In January the new leaves start to push through, followed by pinkish flowers in late February and March. The branches can be brought into the house to speed up the process.

Flowering currant is easy to grow – it is tolerant of most soils and most positions. It can be grown in tubs on the patio or outside the front door and will survive erratic watering. Redcurrant and blackcurrant bushes are of the same family and are also useful. Although they do not bear flowers their fruit can provide additional interest.

Honeysuckle

Honeysuckle provides line material and the longer trails are ideal for graceful downward curves. One of the best honeysuckles to have in the garden is the evergreen *Lonicera japonica* which gives cutting material all the year round except in severe winters. It is easy to establish, it grows quickly and is not fussy as to position.

Honeysuckle flowers during the summer months and many varieties have a charming scent. Altogether it has many attractions, not least the remarkable ability to grow against walls, fences, up trees and over unsightly objects. It is therefore ideal for small growing areas.

For those without a garden the wild deciduous honeysuckle or wood-bine, with fragrant summer flowers, can be found in the countryside.

Eucalyptus

Eucalyptus is line material, evergreen and long-lasting. It is the most widely-available foliage from florists and market stalls. Eucalyptus can easily be grown in the garden and grows amazingly quickly. The young growth with rounded leaves is particularly useful. However, the mature leaves change from a round to a longer ovate shape which is more difficult to use in small designs. It is therefore advisable to prune back each spring to display the distinctive young foliage.

Pittosporum

Pittosporum gives filler material. It also gives wonderful line material for smaller arrangements. *Pittosporum tenuifolium* has shiny wavy-edged leaves, dark stems and small dark purple flowers in the spring. Grown in the garden it provides a neat evergreen bush or small tree and benefits from drastic pruning in spring. It will regenerate freely from the old wood.

The only drawback is that it is not totally hardy and in some areas will therefore suffer badly in severe frosts. It also hates being moved. It is, however, one of the few foliages that flower shops do stock most months of the year and is reasonably priced. One variegated form has pale green leaves with cream edges. It is an absolute stunner both in the garden and in any arrangement. The slightly larger *Pittosporum tobira* can be purchased in a green or variegated form from many florists.

Variegated leaves are those which are composed of at least two colours, e.g. yellow and green or cream and green. These are a great boon to flower arrangers. They liven any design and can take the place of flowers. Many shrubs have variegated varieties such as ivy, periwinkle and holly.

As you become more experienced, your appreciation of the different textures, colours and forms of foliage will grow and you may find that you build up a larger list of shrubs which you find important to yourself as an individual.

Flowers

Flower arrangers' gardens, unless vast, tend to have foliage predominating as flowers are often purchased from a florist with whom they have built up a good relationship. Market stalls can offer good buys, but sometimes care has to be taken to ensure that the flowers are of a good quality. The following flowers are readily available from florists throughout the year. They are not expensive, are good natured and provide a stepping stone to further experimentation and individualism.

If you are unsure about which flowers to buy, look at the flowers available and choose a few stems of a roundish flower, a few of line and a few of filler; the number you buy depending on the size of arrangement you wish to create. Help with colour is given in chapter 13.

Generally speaking you should buy flowers which:

- Show some colour in their buds or they may not develop properly;
- Do not have loose yellow pollen on the flowers as this means they are nearing the end of their lives;
- Have fresh green foliage.

Double flowers will last longer than their single relations.

Cow parsley (Queen Anne's lace)

Although only available for a few months of the year in spring and early summer, cow parsley has to be included. It is a filler. It grows on waste land, riverbanks, in fields, in hedgerows and on motorway verges. It is never far away and available to all. If a weed is a nuisance then cow parsley is not a weed. Many florists now sell dill, a rich man's cow parsley, but it only offers a longer availability. If conditioned well, cow parsley will last for at least five days. Cut short it can be added to table arrangements or, with longer stems, to pedestals. It will always give lightness and joy without charge.

Spray carnations

Because of their strong stems and neat flowers spray carnations are mainly used as line material to reinforce shapes established by the foliage. In tiny arrangements single flowers can be used as focal flowers. Spray carnations are the most popular bought flower and look much better if 'arranged'. They offer exceptional value. If purchased fresh and then properly treated, they can last for weeks. An added bonus is that their side-shoots can be used separately, as filler foliage in your arrangement. When purchasing check that:

- The calyx or cup at the petal base is green, not yellow or brown, and has not split.
- The foliage is a fresh green.
- Several flowers are showing on each stem.
- The buds are plump and firm because small buds which you can squash flat between your fingers will not develop. (You will need a good relationship with your florist to do this!)
- The stems are reasonably long.
- The bottom half of the stem has not been stripped of foliage.
- Spray and standard carnations are extra sensitive to ethylene gas which causes a rapid deterioration of flowers. This gas is given off by fruit and vegetables, so avoid purchasing them from green-grocers unless the fruit and flowers are well segregated.

Chrysanthemums

The single varieties are useful to give focal flowers. The 'blooms' (large single heads) look wonderful in large pedestal arrangements in the autumn. Their disadvantage is that the leaves are not particularly attractive and never last as long as the flowers. So use these flowers with other foliage.

Points to watch when purchasing are:

- The centres of the singles should be predominantly green. Too much yellow means that too much pollen has been released. This only happens when the flower is nearing the end of its lifecycle. The centres of the double varieties should be tight and incurving.
- Avoid any whose leaves have already been removed by the florist. Although the foliage usually deteriorates before the flowers, it does mean they have been in stock too long. Also avoid any whose stem ends are mushy. The leaves and stems should be dark green.
- The petals at the back of the flower head should be crisp and not falling.

- Think twice about purchasing when the secondary stems are really short, especially if they are to be used in a small arrangement. It does not mean that the flowers are inferior, but it does mean that their short stems will be more difficult to divide and use in a small arrangement.

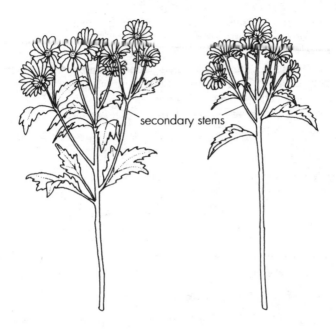

Chrysanthemums with varying lengths of secondary stems

Roses

Rose buds are line material; the flowers are focal. Florists' roses are available all the year round. In the summer they are particularly good value. Although more expensive during the winter months they give that hint of extravagance. Roses are more expensive the longer the stem. For small to medium-sized arrangements, flower arrangers usually reduce the length of the stems. It is thus sometimes worth buying short-stemmed roses from a market stall. Long-lasting spray roses have been introduced recently and are becoming increasingly popular. They can be used in a similar way to spray carnations.

Points to watch when purchasing are:

- Check the fullness of the rose head. Sometimes the outer petals, which droop first, are pulled off to rejuvenate the flower.
- Check that there are no markings at the top of the stem just beneath the flower head. Any dark discoloration shows a weakness and the flower may droop after purchase.
- The foliage should be fresh, crisp, dark green and still firmly attached to the stems.
- The stem ends should not be discoloured and look 'cooked'. If they do, it means the stem ends have been placed briefly in hot water to revive them. This is an acceptable practice but it does mean the flowers could be susceptible to wilting.
- The buds should have burst properly. If no colour is showing, the bud may well not open.

Freesias

Freesias provide filler material. They are usually sold in bunches of five. They are popular because just five stems can give a freshness and fragrance to any arrangement. Remember to remove the dead flowers to encourage those further up the stem to open. It is rare however for every flower to open, even on a top quality stem.

Points to watch when purchasing are:

- Only buy them if at least one flower has opened or is just about to open on each comb and the second and third buds show colour. Otherwise the flowering parts will not develop fully. This is particularly likely to happen during the winter months.
- Ensure that the cellophane wrapping has not been pulled tight over the heads of the freesia. Often this happens with careless handling. Restricted air around the heads of the flowers encourages the germination of botrytis, a grey mould fatal to the long life of cut flowers.
- The stems should be firm.

Alstroemeria

Alstroemeria as filler material is becoming more and more popular, for it is long lasting and very pretty. It can easily be grown in the garden or in tubs. It will flower year after year if left undisturbed. Some types of alstroemeria can survive in very neglected gardens, and become so prolific that they become weeds. Not too much of a problem!

When purchasing ensure that:

- The leaves are a good green and show no signs of turning yellow.
- The stems are strong and do not bend too loosely.

Gypsophila

Gypsophila is a filler. It is one of the most well-known flowers, available from most florists twelve months of the year. In arranging it is often over-used giving a fussy effect. However, used with care it can bring a lightness and brightness to your designs.

Points to watch when you are choosing your gypsophila:

- The stems should be strong and green and have no slime on the ends under water.
- The stems should not be tangled and broken.
- The flower heads dry well on the stems and can be used for dried arrangements but when buying them fresh ensure that the flowers are still alive.

Bulb flowers

Bulb flowers are inexpensive and one of the best indicators that spring is on the way, even though new production techniques mean they are now around much longer.

Key points to watch when purchasing are that:

- The buds of iris, lilies and tulips show flower colour.
- The leaves and buds are not discoloured and do not have brown spots.
- Daffodils are all in bud and that the buds are slightly bent on the stems.

Conditioning

The first objective to establish is the right plant material for your needs and where it can be found. However, if you are to give time and thought to arranging flowers attractively it is important that the flowers do not wilt or die before the end of their natural cut life. The process by which this is done is called *conditioning*.

Plant material dies prematurely if bacteria enters the stem. Bacteria are produced in dirty water, dirty buckets, dirty containers and on dirty scissors. It is therefore of utmost importance that all your components and implements are spotlessly clean so that your plant material can last the maximum length of time possible.

Points to observe

Plant material from the florist has usually been well conditioned but the same simple procedure given below is advisable once stem ends have been out of water.

1　The bottom few centimetres (plus or minus depending on the length of stem) should be removed on the slant with a sharp clean pair of florists' scissors. (Florists use a sharp knife but for many this is difficult to use efficiently.) This diagonal cut exposes the largest amount of inner tissue and it is this tissue which contains the vessels taking water up to the flowers and leaves. It also prevents a heavy stem end forming a seal against the container. Remove any leaves which would go below the water line, as long term submersion causes decomposition and the spread of bacteria.

2　The cut stem ends should be placed immediately in a bucket or container of deep warm water and left in a cool place for at least two hours. A warm liquid travels more quickly than a cool one because it has less air in it – think of the viscosity of treacle before and after the tin has been placed in a saucepan of hot water. The two exceptions to this rule are chrysanthemums and bouvardia which need cool water. The water should be deep because a certain amount of water can also enter the plant through the length of the stem.

　　The plant material should be left in a cool place because more water evaporates through the pores on the leaves when the atmosphere is warmer or drier. This is also why arrangements should be placed away from draughts, central heating and the heat given out by televisions. The water is needed in the stem, not in the atmosphere.

3   All bulb flowers should have their stem ends cut off. The whitish stem ends of daffodils and tulips should be removed as water does not travel up this section as easily. All bulb flowers last longer in shallow rather than deep water. Their stems generally are softer and thicker than other flowers and are therefore easier to place on a pinholder than in foam. Daffodils secrete a sticky substance poisonous to other flowers, but if they are left on their own in water for 24 hours they can then be arranged with other flowers. Wipe the stem ends gently but do not recut them.

4   When your plant material has been arranged keep the arrangement topped up with water.

From the garden

The foliage from deciduous shrubs (those which lose their leaves in winter) always lasts longer when picked later in the season when it is more mature and has stronger cells than earlier in the year, but obviously not in the autumn when it is preparing to lose its leaves. Flowers and foliage from the garden should ideally be collected in the evening. By this time the maximum reserves of food will be stored in the plant to be used during the hours of darkness. The cool of evening also means that little moisture is being lost through the leaves. If possible take a bucket with a little water in it round the garden with you when you are collecting your plant material.

Research into prolonging the life of flowers shows that hammering stem ends or making an upward slit in the stem ends – a long established practice – only causes harm. The ensuing damage to cell tissue encourages the rapid growth of bacteria and thus reduces the life of the plant material. Similarly, if you are removing thorns from roses, great care should be taken that the stem is not damaged, thus allowing bacteria to enter.

If your garden foliage grows in an urban area, wash it in a little washing up liquid to take off the grime. Ideally leave the more mature foliage to soak for 20–60 minutes, but demands on the kitchen sink or the bath often make this impractical. Note that some foliage can get waterlogged with too long a soak. Rinse the foliage well before leaving it for at least a couple of hours in warm water in a cool place.

Tips and treatments

If you are conditioning silver or grey foliage such as senecio or *Cineraria maritima*, do not submerge it. The effect of grey is given by myriad grey hairs which get waterlogged on submersion. They never recover. Interestingly, grey and silver foliage is more resilient to water shortages than most green foliage, as the hairs reflect strong light and reduce water evaporation. Some other types of plants which can withstand dry conditions are those with:

- Many very small leaves;
- Green woody stems;
- Thick waxy leaf surfaces.

Perhaps this will be useful knowledge if our climate continues to become warmer.

Sugar added to the water is sometimes recommended as food for the plants but bacteria love it too, so do not use it. Some swear by a combination of sugar and bleach – one to counteract the demerits of the other. Plant food is a lot easier to add, is more effective and is probably cheaper. It can be easily purchased and is sometimes given free of charge when you are buying flowers from a florist. If added to the warm water in a clean bucket the special formula prevents the rapid increase of bacteria and helps the flowers and foliage to develop to their full potential. The water should not be changed, only added to. There are special formulae for cut flowers, for shrub and tree cut stems and there is one which allows you to mix daffodils with other cut flowers.

Plants have long been known to make their own aspirin. The latest scientific research seems to show that aspirin helps stimulate a plant's defence mechanism, so adding a small amount of aspirin to the water may indeed help to defend the plant against bacteria.

Copper and brass containers emit toxic poisons which combat bacteria, but it is almost impossible to keep the inside of these containers as clean as you could glass, plastic or ceramic. So try adding a shining copper coin to an inner container within your copper or brass container.

Ethylene gas shortens the life of cut plant material. Unfortunately it is given off by numerous forms of life, in particular fruit and vegetables and decaying plant material. This is why you should remove the dying heads on a flower spray and keep flowers which are particularly susceptible, such as carnations, gypsophila and orchids, away from fruit and vegetables. Unfortunately fruit and vegetables cannot be used to hasten the blooming of tight buds for a special occasion. Many of the flowers would only shrivel or drop. They would not develop to their full potential.

There are other treatments for specific plant material, but these you will find in appendix 3.

For the moment this is all the information that you need. Do remember to add water to your container daily and, if the atmosphere is dry, spray your arrangement.

You have the foliage, you have the flowers. The next chapter looks at what to put them in and how to keep them there.

2
—————— EQUIPMENT ——————

Only the very minimum expense is needed to start arranging flowers. There are many wonderful containers and vases available to the discerning eye. After reading this book and trying out the designs you may wish to start scouring charity shops, raiding skips and being the first in the queue at the sales with a view to increasing the variety of arrangements which you will soon feel confident to try on your own.

The word *mechanics* is flower-arranging terminology for all the equipment and materials which keep stems in place. (Wire netting, which is also a mechanic, is not mentioned until later.) Most of the mechanics and containers you will need for the practical work in this book can be adapted from household items.

—————— Sundries ——————

Many garden centres and DIY garden superstores now sell florists' sundries, usually presented on large display stands. Often, but not always, florists will sell you these items. However, the best source is likely to be your local flower club. Besides being the meeting place of like-minded individuals it will give you a chance to learn more about flowers and most clubs have sales tables where all the items in this chapter can usually be bought at extremely reasonable prices. Details of your nearest flower club can be obtained from NAFAS (The National Association of Flower Arrangement Societies of Great Britain) at 21 Denbigh Street, London SW1V 2HF. (Do enclose a s.a.e.) Your local club will also be able to inform you of flower arranging classes in the area.

For now the following are recommended:

- Floral foam – the first and most widely known trade name is Oasis
- Green plastic containers to take the foam
- Candlecup
- Oasisfix
- Frogs (four prongs on a disc that hold foam in place)
- Florists' tape
- Candleholder
- Scissors
- Pinholder
- A base

Floral foam

Although *floral foam* comes under several brand names, such as Oasis and Triflora, there are only two distinct types, green foam and brown or grey foam.

Green foam

Green foam is soaked in water and then used for fresh plant material. Floral foam was invented by a chemist called Vernon Smithers in the early 1940s, quite by mistake. Flower arrangers today would now find life much more difficult if they were restricted to pinholders and wire netting. Floral foam is light, inexpensive and is made of resins which restrict the growth of bacteria so that the flowers last longer. For many flower arrangers the greatest advantage that foam gives is that it enables stems to be inserted at all angles. Plant material can be angled downwards to hide the rim of the container and to give graceful flow to a design. It is therefore vital, whatever the container or design, that the foam rises at least 2.5 cm above the rim for smaller arrangements and 5 cm for larger arrangements. Pare a little foam off the sharp angles with a knife to soften the shape. This is called *chamfering*.

Do not use too much foam. The more you use, the more you will have to hide. Approximate amounts of foam to use are given with each arrangement. You will soon have a feel for how much you need.
Foam comes in bricks and in cylinders. A brick should be immersed

under water for 100 seconds and a cylinder for about 60 seconds. Do not 'plunge' foam under water. The brick should be allowed to sink under its own weight. However, do not oversoak at this point or the foam will tend to crumble when you insert your stems. Add additional water to the container to give a reservoir after the flowers have been arranged.

Foam can be re-used by simply turning it over and using the other side. However, avoid using a piece of foam with too many holes. It can be very frustrating when inserting the last stem to find that the network of tunnels has united and thus threatens to cause collapse. Once used foam must not be allowed to dry out. It can be kept moist for months, even years, if placed in a plastic bag which is firmly tied. If it does dry out, boiling water, with a little added liquid soap, should be poured over the foam. It can then be re-used but it will not retain water as efficiently as the fresh. Do remember to top up with water daily.

Brown or grey foam

Brown or grey foam is used solely for dried plant material and cannot be saturated with water. It is much harder and less crumbly than green foam.

Green plastic containers

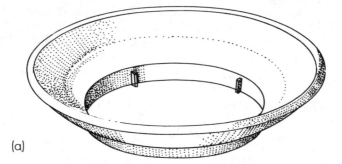

(a)

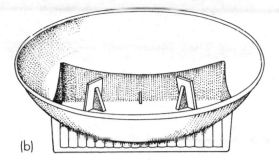

(b)

These two dishes will enable you to create a wide variety of designs. They are especially useful for table arrangements. Do not worry if you cannot find them at your garden centre – any small shallow receptacle which retains water will do. Examples of these alternative containers, adapted from household items, are given in each chapter. However, the purpose-designed plastic containers are particularly good because:

- They have been especially designed so that in (*a*) a cylinder of foam and in (*b*) a section of a brick of foam will fit snugly and securely.
- They can be purchased in a dull green colour with a flat texture. (Do not buy white ones unless you are able to spray them a more inconspicuous colour as they are difficult to disguise and will dominate your plant material.)
- They are unbreakable.
- They are cheap.

Candlecup

Empty bottles and candlesticks are often used as containers for graceful, raised arrangements. All you need in order to adapt them for flower arranging is a *candlecup*. This is a plastic bowl with a protruding knob to insert in the neck of a bottle or candlestick. Usually there are two sizes available. The smaller size is ideal for smaller, more delicate designs and the larger one for when you have an abundance of plant material. The two most widely available colours are white and black, but they can easily be sprayed. Not all bottle necks are wide enough to take the candlecup, but many are. To keep it secure and happy you will need some Oasisfix.

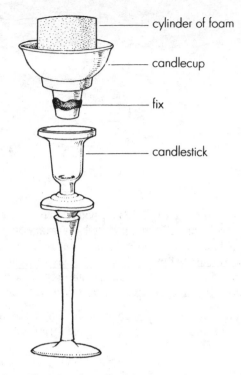

A candlecup and candlestick

Oasisfix

This is similar to Blutac, Plasticine or chewing gum and indeed these can be used. *Oasisfix*, or *fix* as we will now call it, is used when two hard surfaces need to be held together securely but not permanently. A small piece needs to be worked and warmed in the hands before use to make it more malleable. It can only be used to good effect when the two surfaces to be held together are dry and dustfree. A thin sausage of fix can be wrapped round the protruding knob of the candle-cup to ensure good contact between the inside of the bottle neck and the cup.

Fix is difficult to remove because it is sticky, so if you are using a silver or brass candlestick, protect it by using a strip of Sellotape against the metal. The fix is then making contact with the Sellotape and the candlecup and not the metal and the candlecup. Fix is also used with frogs.

Frogs

An unusual name for an item that bears no resemblance to an amphibian! A *frog* is a round plastic disc with four prongs.

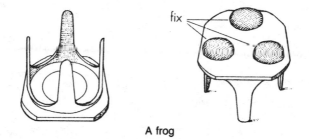

fix

A frog

It is used to secure foam to a container which has not been specifically designed to take its shape, e.g. a paté dish. Three small knobs of kneaded fix should be pressed on to the dry, dustfree undersurface of the frog at regular intervals. One knob alone would slightly disturb the balance. The frog and fix are then placed firmly in position in the container. Your piece of foam is then placed on the prongs of the frog.

Another way to secure the foam, which can be used for additional safety especially if you are creating a large arrangement, is to use florists' tape.

Florists' tape

This is a strong adhesive tape, purchased on a roll, which sticks firmly to foam. The ends should be wrapped round the container to keep the foam and container as one. Avoid using too many widths across the foam as this will limit the space for stems. When creating a symmetrical design, use the tape off-centre as the central area will need to be free for the placement of stems. Unlike Sellotape it does not lose its adhesion when wet.

Candleholders

Candles can be inserted into an arrangement and kept in place with cocktail sticks or wires, but specially-designed plastic *candleholders* keep them the most secure.

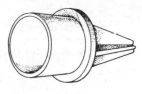

A candleholder

Their special design keeps the breaking up of the foam to the absolute minimum when they are inserted. If the candle is to be lit, it is best to buy a candleholder with a metal insert. Alternatively, line the holder with metal foil. If the candle is too slim for the holder and the candle wobbles, wedge it with newspaper or a little fix.

Scissors

Buying a good pair of *floral scissors* is expensive but essential. Household scissors will only frustrate you, squash the stems and perhaps cut your fingers. Scissors need to have short blades, a serrated inner edge and, for preference, a hole to allow the easy cutting of thicker stems. They must also be easy to grasp.

When buying a pair, check if there is enough room for your fingers and thumb to fit comfortably in the handles.

Pinholders

Pinholders come in many shapes and sizes. Only one pinholder is necessary for beginners and indeed for many more advanced arrangers. The most useful size is probably 2.5″ in diameter (6.25 cm) but 2″ or 3″ (5 cm or 7.50 cm) would be fine. Pinholder manufacturers have decided not to go metric in the forseeable future so the imperial measurement still stands. A pinholder is not needed until chapter 8 for the upward crescent design.

Pinholders do not vary much in price but they do in quality. It is therefore important that you verify that:

• The pins are brass and not steel. Brass pins are yellow, steel are grey. Brass pins do not rust; steel pins do.

- The base should be lead and feel heavy in the hand. This weight gives stability to your arrangement. Pinholders attached to plastic suckers are not a good investment.
- The pins should be close together and firmly embedded in the lead.

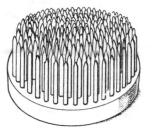

A pinholder

Avoid placing foam directly onto a pinholder. It is extremely difficult to remove all traces later unless you place a piece of old nylon stocking onto the pins first.

Bases

A *base* is the term used for anything on which a flower arrangement stands. It is not essential but is desirable because it:

- Protects the furniture from any drops of water or condensation.
- Gives visual stability, especially when the container seems too small for the plant material and the effect is top heavy. Conversely do not use a base if the container already appears big.
- Links with the colour of the flowers – and perhaps also with the colour scheme of the room – to give overall unity to the arrangement in its setting.

Bases are simple to find, adapt or make. Simple but effective bases are breadboards, glass cheese and butter plates, table mats, wood slices cut on the cross, cork boards, teapot stands or plain trays. The smooth round or oval shaped bases work better than those which are square or rectangular and thus angular, unless the container is also angular. Perhaps the most useful is made of fibre board. Fibre board bases can be bought from flower club sales tables or can be purchased from a DIY or wood shop where you can choose the dimensions. Alternatively use a cake board. The two most useful boards would be a round one of approximately 30 cm diameter and an oval one of approximately 35 cm diameter longways.

A good colour for a base is a soft green, the flower arranger's neutral colour which harmonises with everything. However, to hide the bare board you need to sew a cover. The easiest material for non-expert seamstresses to tackle is a thin man-made fibre with a light give or stretch to it, such as nylon jersey. Using the chosen base as a template, mark the outline shape of the material allowing an extra 5 cm. Turn a small amount of the material under and sew round firmly. Make a hem large enough to take a thin strip of running elastic. Place the base on the back of the material and pull the elastic drawstring until the mob-cap firmly covers the base. Tie the elastic and tuck the ends inside the hem.

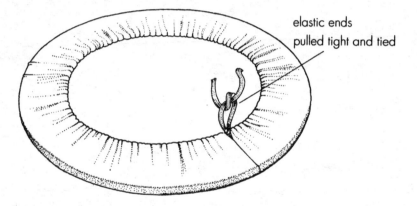

elastic ends
pulled tight and tied

A round base

You now have all the basics to enable you to start the actual flower arranging. By being well prepared you will find that flower arranging is much easier than you ever believed possible.

3

TABLE ARRANGEMENTS

Table arrangements for sit-down meals should be either tall enough to see under or low enough to see over. In Victorian times in large homes, the taller arrangements were much in evidence, overflowing with ferns, trails of ivy and a profusion of flowers. Today the size of our homes and perhaps the increased pressures in our lives call for a smaller, low arrangement that can be created easily yet is effective and worthy of admiration. It is said that the arrangements for tables where the guests are seated should be no more than 28 cm high. However if your guests are on the Amazonian side, there is no reason for the arrangement not to be taller provided that conversation will not be stilted because vision is obscured.

A table arrangement should be in good proportion to the size of the table. As a very rough guide no more than one fifth of the table should be covered. If the table is large, perhaps for more than 10 people, two smaller arrangements are more practical and can be enjoyed by all. The two could perhaps be linked by a trail of ivy.

Plant material used for table arrangements should be in top condition for the very good reason that it will be subjected to scrutiny over several hours. A caterpillar on a half-eaten leaf would not assist enjoyment of the meal.

Your table centre should be part of the overall effect created by your table setting. Choose flowers which will repeat a colour in your china or pottery and which will harmonise with the table linen. If the occasion is grand, choose more sophisticated flowers such as orchids and lilies.

If the setting is informal, perhaps in the kitchen, choose relaxed flowers such as daisy chrysanthemums, anemones or flowers from the garden.

There are various rules that apply particularly to certain styles of arrangement. One rule that applies to all designs in this section is that all stems must appear to originate from one point in the foam which will be called point X. The first stem is placed in the foam to establish the height of the arrangement. This stem would appear to originate from deeper in the foam than it actually does. (Remember that you insert the minimum length of stem.) All your other stems must appear to radiate from this imaginary point X. They do not but they should give the impression that they do. This imaginary point is marked on many of the drawings in this chapter. This 'rule' is particularly important and will therefore be mentioned regularly.

Remember that for good visual balance, stronger forms which are your focal flowers need to be placed well within the limits of your design established by the line material (see page 6). As table arrangements are to be viewed from all angles, focal material should be placed at intervals round the design. Place some on shorter stems closer to the foam to give a three-dimensional effect and thus more interest. This is called *recessing* the plant material.

In this chapter, approximate lengths of plant material are given to set you on your way. You will soon have the confidence to set your own parameters.

—— All round or circular design —— for a round table

Components

The components are as follows:

- A cylinder of foam.
- A round shallow container about 10 cm in diameter. This could be the green plastic bowl especially designed to take a cylinder of foam as described in chapter 2. Alternatively the lid of a coffee jar, a guinea-pig bowl, a small round foil dish, a small round margarine tub (if the tub is too deep, reduce its height with scissors) or a flowerpot saucer. Any container can be used as long as it will hold water, will not leak and can have the cylinder of foam firmly strapped to it. Alternatively you can use a frog and fix to keep your foam firmly secured.
- Line material, such as small-leaved ivy sprays, privet, rosemary, eucalyptus.
- Line flowers, such as spray carnations, are wonderful for this design. Three stems should be sufficient (bearing about 15 flowers and buds). If flowering line material is used, e.g. blossom, these might not be needed.
- Concealer leaves, such as ivy, geranium, flowering currant. About 6–9 depending on their size.
- Focal material, such as single chrysanthemums. These flowers should not be more than two times larger than the other flowers used or they will be too big and your design will not have all parts 'belonging' to each other. Try not to use bulb flowers, such as iris, daffodils or tulips – they are uncomfortable in foam. If bulb flowers are the only flowers available, make a hole in the foam with a strong stem or short piece of dowelling before inserting the soft stem of your bulb flower. If you are choosing spray chrysanthemums, check that the secondary stems are long enough to be used individually. One or two stems of spray chrysanthemums should be sufficient (see pages 15–16).
- Filler material, such as cow parsley, geranium flowers, rosehips, berries, pittosporum, *Viburnum tinus*, London pride, alstroemeria, gypsophila – one or more varieties according to your taste.

Method

1 Place the foam in the dish and secure well. The foam should have been soaked as described in chapter 2. The foam should rise about 5 cm above the container.

2 Place a stem of line foliage centrally, in position (*a*) below. For your first attempt use line material which rises approximately 12 cm above the level of the foam. Only insert the minimum length of stem, otherwise you will find the stems crossing each other at a later stage and the foam breaking up. Ensure that the length of stem inserted into the foam is free of leaves or knobs as these also break up the foam.

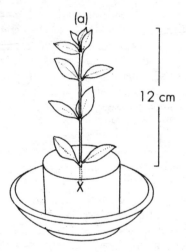

(*a*)

12 cm

X

3 Place an odd number of stems in position (*b*) opposite, (still using the same line material as this is a small arrangement and will look confused if material is mixed at this stage) out of the sides of the foam at regular intervals. They should be about two thirds the length of the first placement, i.e. about 8 cm from the foam. Resist the temptation to make them longer. If the line material is slim, more will be needed than if broader line material is used. Five to seven stems is usually the right number. These stems should be inserted about half way up the foam and angled slightly downwards over the rim of the container. Angle them so that they appear to originate from point X. This is very important.

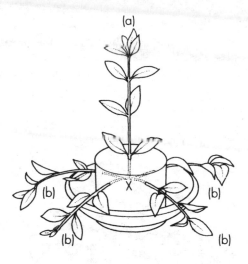

4 Place an odd number of stems (*c*), with the stem length the same as for (*b*), out of the top of the foam. Avoid placing these directly above the material which you have already inserted. Place them in between. It is very important that these stems stay within the boundaries of the dotted line triangle shown below. If they do not, reduce their length where necessary. Check that all stems appear to come from the same point of origin (X) within the foam.

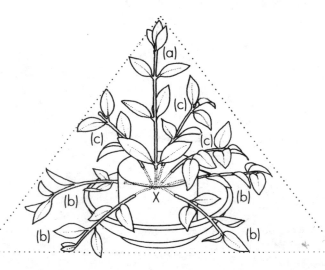

5   At this stage add concealer leaves to cover some of the foam and
dish rim. Avoid a frilly effect by inserting stems so that the leaves
lie at different angles. Vary the stem lengths slightly. Work *through*
the design, not just around the rim. Think of the whole.

6   Now add line flowers almost to the limits of the design and throughout the design. Place your first line flower so that it stops just

short of your first central line foliage placement. Always keep within the triangle created by the line foliage. Place these stems at regular intervals to avoid wide open spaces. They should all appear to radiate from the same point X. Angle some downwards over the rim in between the outline foliage.

Line flowers can always be added after you have placed the line foliage and before you add concealer material if you prefer.

7 Place the focal flowers at intervals around the arrangement. The larger the flowers, the lower they should be in the arrangement for good stability. They should also be closer to the foam and therefore on shorter stems. This *recessing* will give more interest to your design. The viewer will thus look at it longer. Again avoid a 'frill'. If possible angle your stems so that the flowers look natural. To avoid the design becoming bottom heavy, place some smaller focal flowers or developing buds higher in the design.

8 Add filler material to complete (see over). Keep within the framework established by the line material. Sometimes only very little filler material is necessary. Perhaps a few more line flowers are needed. Add water to your bowl. Try to ensure that there is always a little in the bottom of your container.

Later you can try creating a larger design for a larger table – for example 18 cm high. The other line material should be two thirds of this length, approximately 12 cm.

The all-round arrangement

—— Horizontal table arrangement —— for an oval or rectangular table

Components

The components are as follows:

- One third of a brick of foam. The foam must rise about 5 cm above the rim of the container.
- A shallow container. This could be the green plastic bowl especially designed for part of a block of foam. If you use a paté dish, or large ashtray or a foil dish you will also need a frog and fix and/or tape.
- Line material, e.g. small-leaved ivy sprays, privet, rosemary, honeysuckle or light branches of blossom.
- Line flowers – say five stems of spray carnations (these may not be needed if blossom is used).
- Concealer leaves, e.g. round ivy leaves, geraniums, flowering currant, tolmeia – about eight to twelve depending on size.

- Focal material – three stems of spray chrysanthemums or perhaps seven small to medium roses (not in tight bud).
- Filler material, e.g. *Viburnum tinus*, skimmia, cow parsley, freesia or alstroemeria.

Method

1   Place the foam in the dish and secure well. The foam should have been soaked as described in chapter 2.
2   Place a stem of line foliage centrally, in position (*a*) as shown below. For your first attempt use line material that rises 12 cm above the level of the foam. Only insert the minimum length of stem. Ensure that the stem end is clean and free of bumps.
3   Place two stems of the same line material in both long ends of the foam, position (*b*), a third longer than stem (*a*), i.e. approximately 16 cm long. You have now formed the triangle ABC. BC is about 42 cm long (2 × 16 cm plus 10 cm for the width of the foam). Therefore your completed arrangement will be about 42 cm long.

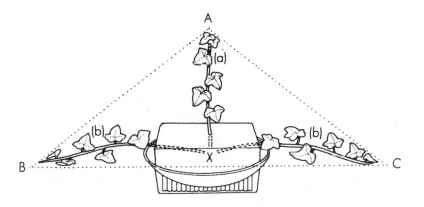

4   Place two short pieces of line foliage in position (*c*) as shown on the next page. Repeat on the other side. These pieces should be approximately half the length of (*b*), i.e. 8 cm from the foam. At this point check that every stem appears to have the same point of origin (X). There should be approximately the same spacing between all the lower placements.

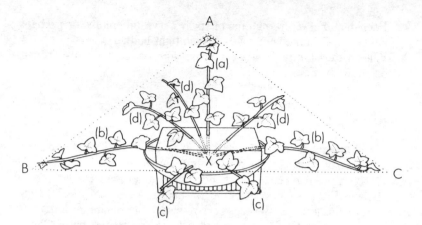

5 Place an odd number of stems (*d*) in the top and sides of the foam as in the illustration above. They should be about the same length as (*c*) – approximately 8 cm long. Do not have any material protruding outside the dotted line triangle. Recheck that all stems appear to come from the same point of origin. Place stems (*d*) above the spaces between the lower placements and not directly in a line above them.

6 Add concealer leaves to cover some of the foam and dish rim. Avoid a frilly effect by inserting stems at different angles. Work the design from all angles.

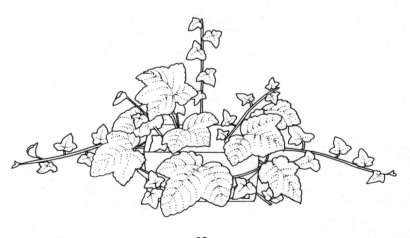

7 Add line flowers almost to the limits of the design and throughout the design. Place the first flower so that it reinforces the first vertical placement of line foliage. Always keep within the triangle. Place the stems at regular intervals to avoid wide spaces. Pay particular attention to the area between placements (*b*) and (*c*) to ensure that the material forms a smooth shape. Add extra line material to the limits of your ABC triangle if this is necessary.

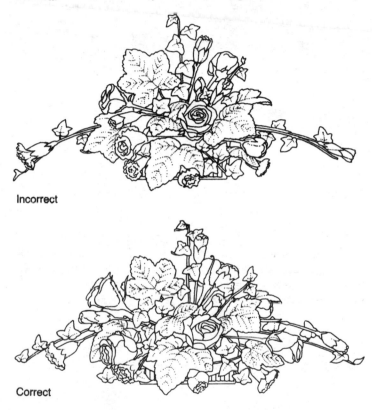

Incorrect

Correct

8 Place the focal flowers at intervals round the arrangement. Avoid a tendency to have an all-round arrangement with two arms attached as shown above by graduating the size of your flowers carefully so that the arrangement has unity. The smallest focal flowers should be closer to the edges, the largest in the centre and the others in between. Alternatively use more line flowers.

9 Add filler material to complete. Keep within the framework established by the line material.

The completed horizontal arrangement

10 Ensure that your arrangement always has a little water in the bottom of your container.

Next time, why not experiment with different plant material or a larger design? For a larger design place a stem 15 cm long to establish the height. Now use stems 18 cm long for the horizontal line with the other plant material 9 cm in length. The overall length of your table arrangement will be 46 cm (2 × 18 cm plus 10 cm).

4
── THE DOWNWARD ──
CRESCENT

The downward crescent is light and graceful. It gives a sophisticated arrangement using the minimal amount of plant material. As it is always displayed in a raised container it can be placed where space is at a premium, such as on a buffet table. Raised containers have been mentioned in chapter 2. There are many effective raised containers especially designed for flower arrangers but there are also many alternatives. A glass bottle can be used or better still a candlestick. Heavy containers do not work so well. This is a light design and if your container is made from heavy material, such as pottery, ensure that it has a slim shape. A bottle can be filled with water to give extra stability. A few drops of food colouring could be added to the water to harmonise with the flowers you use.

Your container needs to be between 20 cm and 32 cm high. An arrangement on a 20 cm tall container will use smaller-sized material than one 32 cm high. Trails of the neat goldheart ivy, cornflowers, pinks and *Alchemilla mollis* would be in scale with the 20 cm container but could be small in relation to a 32 cm candlestick where the larger ivies and generous garden roses would be more appropriate.

A candlecup should be securely attached to your container with fix and adhesive tape.

Candles and flowers harmonise well and this design is suited to the inclusion of a candle. To support the candle you will need a candleholder as mentioned in chapter 2. If you find this hard to track down, the following is a good alternative. Place a piece of adhesive tape, sticky side uppermost, on a firm surface. Place four cocktail sticks at regular intervals on the tape. Wrap the tape round the base of the candle with the long ends well protruding. Push these ends, which should be at least 2.5 cm long, into the foam.

When you are choosing candles look for those which are long and reasonably slender. Make sure that they are not chipped or broken, though a polish with a duster can work wonders on a sad candle. If you have time, put your candles in the deep freeze or fridge for 24 hours before using them. They will burn much more slowly.

Whatever the colour of your candle, repeat this colour in your design. As a general rule use plainly-shaped candles in a muted colour – cream, soft green or pale pink. These colours harmonise well with plant material. Lighted candles can of course be a hazard so never leave a lighted candle in an empty room.

If a candle is to be used in this or any other arrangement ensure that the plant material does not come further than half way up the candle. So if you are using a candle in a horizontal table arrangement which is 15 cm tall you will need a 30 cm candle.

A candle looks delightful in the table arrangements in chapter 3. Just follow the same principles.

If candlelight is going to be the means of illumination, use light coloured flowers in your designs. Dark colours disappear in the subdued light of candles, so avoid dark blues, violets and dark green foliage. Use instead colours that have a tint of white in them – the pastel shades.

Components

The components are as follows:

- A cylinder of foam. The foam must rise at least 2.5 cm above the rim of the container. A larger piece cut from a block of foam may be used for larger designs.
- A raised container, candlestick or bottle with candlecup.
- A candleholder or cocktail sticks and florists' tape (optional).
- A candle (optional).
- Curved line material (this design will not work with straight line material) such as sprays of ivy, rosemary, eucalyptus or broom.
- Line flowers, with a curved or thin flexible stem. A stem of spray carnations can easily be pruned to make a curve. These may not be needed if blossom or flowering line foliage is used for the outline.
- Concealer leaves such as round ivy leaves, geranium or tolmeia.
- Focal material. Spray chrysanthemums are ideal for this design. Alternatively you could try using roses.
- Filler material such as pittosporum, freesia, alstroemeria, gypsophila, skimmia or *Viburnum tinus*.

Method

1 Place the foam in the container and secure well.
2 Insert the candleholder in the centre of the foam and place the candle in the holder.
3 Place a piece of line material (a) centrally to reach no more than half way up the candle, as shown over the page.
4 Insert curved line material into the sides of the foam so that it flows downwards (b). The stems should be inserted in the top half of the foam and angled downwards. You have now formed the triangle ABC. Each downward stem should be about twice the length of (a). If straightened they will also be approximately the same length as the container's height. The curve in the stem and the angle at which they are placed will mean they fall well short of the base.
5 Add shorter stems (c) angled downwards. Their stem ends should appear to have the same imaginary origin X. Repeat on the far side. These should be about one third the length of placements (b). They should just come over the rim of the container and a little beyond.

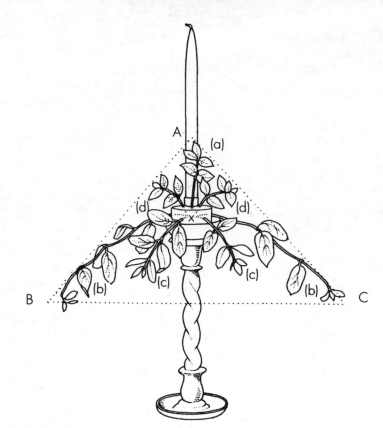

6   Insert short stems (*d*) in the top of the foam, all apparently arising from the same point in the foam (X). Do not go outside the dotted line triangle.

7   Use plain round leaves to conceal the mechanics and to provide a restful contrast to the other material.

8   Take line flowers through the design, stopping short of the boundaries.

9   Insert focal flowers low in the arrangement and slightly recessed. The larger flowers should be placed in the central area graduating outwards to the smallest flowers. If the arrangement is to be placed against a wall, use your best blooms at the front. Wherever an arrangement is to be placed it is always important to have some colour at the back of the design.

10 Add filler material to complete the design. As in the horizontal table arrangement, ensure that the two long stems are not isolated. Graduate the material so that the design has unity. Do not worry if you feel that only a little is needed – you are probably right.

Do not concentrate on one small part of this design before moving on to another area. Always be aware of inserting your stems throughout the design so that as you create all parts belong to the whole.

5

——— SYMMETRICAL ———
TRIANGLE

Symmetrical means that each side of your design, divided by the central stem, is equally balanced. It does not mean that each side is identical but that they are similar. It means that the visual weight on each side is approximately equal, as shown below.

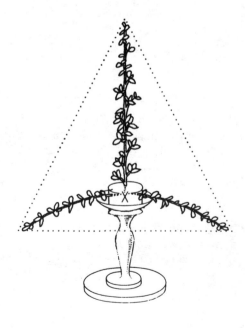

The symmetrical triangle is one of the most useful shapes to create. The pedestal arrangement most commonly used for large rooms, halls and places of worship is simply an enlargement of the traditional triangle. Scaled down it can be created with wild flowers or perhaps alpine or rock garden flowers to give a symmetrical triangle in miniature. In the home it is often placed centrally on a piece of furniture or in an alcove.

More flowers and foliage are used in the symmetrical triangle than in the previous designs in this section. Therefore your mechanics must be extremely secure.

In order to gain the greatest interest in your design allow your flowers to face in all directions. Look at a plant and observe how the flowers and leaves do this. All angles of flowers are interesting and a combination of angles gives variety.

Try not to create a flat arrangement. Depth or a strong three-dimensional form will create interest and hold the eye. Depth can be created in different ways.

One method is not to ignore the back of the arrangement even though it is to be placed against a wall and therefore not visible. The back of your arrangement should always be built up with foliage and flowers. It does not have to contain the best blooms, but the colour in your design must be repeated at the back. Even if little of the colour shows through, its presence can always be felt. This is very important for this design.

Another way to build up the third dimension is to recess some of your flowers and foliage. Shorter stems, usually of bolder plant material, are positioned closer to the foam. Recessing also takes emphasis away from a 'stemmy' effect which is often created by using flowers such as spray carnations and freesias which have a small proportion of flower head to stem.

Different plant material is suggested in the rest of this chapter and thereafter. Further information about them is given in appendices 2, 3 and 4.

Components

The components are as follows:

- A raised container. The flowers need to be raised so that a graceful downward, relaxed effect can be achieved. A flat bowl makes this design too static. Use a low candlestick and large candlecup, a plant pot drip tray stuck with fix to an upside-down plant pot, or the green plastic purpose-made container raised by means of a tin, bowl or even a glass turned upside-down. If you wish to have a large design, make sure that your container will take sufficient foam to hold your stems firmly in place.
- Foam to fit your container, very well secured with a frog and fix and/or a length of sticky tape.
- Line material. If your container is made of glass, use finer line material such as cotoneaster, box or escallonia. If made of sturdier material, pottery perhaps, then strong line material such as camellia or griselinia would be appropriate.
- Line flowers.
- Focal flowers.
- Concealer material, for example fatsia, heuchera, tellima or large ivy leaves.
- Filler material. Both flowers and foliage will be needed. If you are using several varieties of flower, vary the shape of the flower heads.

Method

1 Place a piece of line material (*a*) about one and a half times the height of the container in the top of the foam, centrally and two thirds of the way back.
2 Place stems (*b*), about half the length of (*a*), sideways out of the foam and angled downwards. Ideally they should have a gentle curve. This flow of plant material below the rim of the container prevents the arrangement looking as if it is unhappily perched on a stand. The container and the plant material will become a harmonious whole. This completes the triangle.
3 Add two stems (*c*), approximately half the length of stem (*a*), out of the top of the foam. They must not protrude outside the boundary of the triangle. If they do protrude they must be reduced even if they are only half the length of (*a*).

4   At this point check that all stems are originating from the imaginary point X deep in the foam.

5   Add two short stems (*d*), about half the length of (*b*), at the front and back of the design angled downwards and outwards.

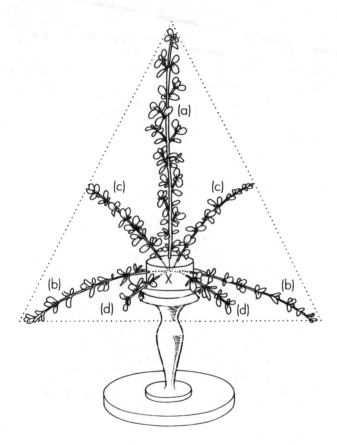

6   Give depth to the design by adding a stem of foliage and/or flowers behind the central stem and angled slightly backwards. This will be shorter than the main stem.

7   Use concealer leaves to cover some of the foam and container rim. Use some leaves on longer stems so that they are not all at the base of the design but taken through the lower half of your triangle.

8 Reinforce this shape with line flowers but do not go beyond the boundaries of the triangle. Take additional line flowers through the design front and back. Remember that longer stems can be used if angled backwards for they then become less dominant and fit within your 'triangle'.

9 Create the focal area with perhaps three carnations or open roses. If you use gerberas, ensure that they do not overpower your design. Do not place your focal flowers too neatly. Only have one full-on. Turn the others slightly to provide more interest.

10 Complete the design with filler flowers and filler foliage. Do not go beyond the boundaries.

The symmetrical triangle arrangement

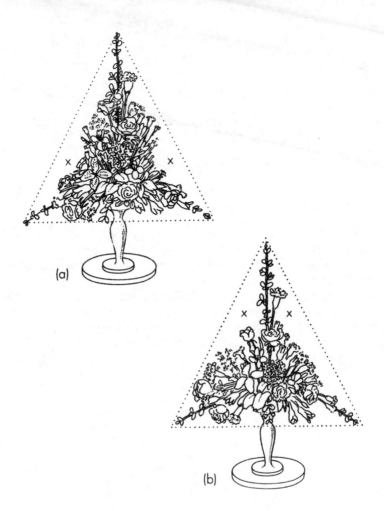

Two examples of incorrectly balanced arrangements

Design *(a)* needs more material at points X. The triangle has not been sufficiently filled. If several stems at points X are angled backwards, more depth and therefore more interest are created. Design *(b)* needs more material at X in the top half of the design. It is now bottom heavy.

6
— ASYMMETRICAL — TRIANGLE

A true asymmetrical triangle is a delight to behold. It is usually positioned on one side of a chest, mantlepiece or table rather than centrally. It is often used to balance an ornament or lamp. It is used a great deal in interpretative show-work where suitable accessories are placed within the design. If the asymmetrical triangle is positioned at an angle, greater depth, and therefore greater interest, is created.

The *symmetrical* triangle has a central stem or axis dividing the triangle ABC into two equal parts.

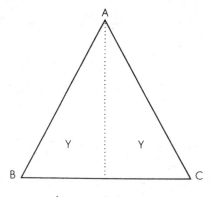

A symmetrical triangle

The central axis of an *asymmetrical* triangle cuts the triangle ABC into two unequal parts. Therefore in the asymmetrical design the material in triangle Y must be made to balance visually the material in triangle Z. This is done in two ways:

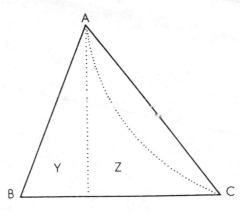

An asymmetrical triangle

- By using heavier, bolder material in Y.
- By scooping out the triangle ABC. The imaginary dotted line shown above forms the limits of your design. Your material will not extend beyond its boundaries.

Components

The components are as follows:

- A flat container. For a small arrangement of less than about 30 cm high you can use the small green dish described in chapter 2. For any larger design use the larger green container or its equivalent.
- The container can be a low, raised container but it must not be too high or have too visible a stem as this will upset your asymmetrical balance. The candlestick used for the downward crescent is much too tall.
- Some foam – one third of a brick if you are using the larger of the two green plastic containers.
- Frog and fix and/or tape.
- Line material. The tallest piece establishing the height should have a gentle curve, such as broom, escallonia, ivy, holly or eucalyptus.
- Concealer leaves. Larger leaves are needed for this design. Bergenia, fatshedera, and many ivy or hosta leaves are ideal.
- Focal flowers.
- Filler material.
- A base.

Method

1   Place the long gently-curved stem (*a*) in the top of the foam, two thirds of the way back and slightly to one side. Angle the stem so that the tip is approximately above where the stem enters the foam. Do not allow the stem tip to go beyond the centre of the foam or it will look as if it is falling over.

2   Place line material (*b*), one third the length of (*a*), out of the front of the foam angled downwards over the rim of the container and away from stem (*a*).

3   Place line material (*c*), half to two thirds the length of (*a*), out of the side of the foam and slightly forwards. You have now formed the triangle ABC, divided by the line AD. Triangle ABD will contain your heavier material, while triangle ADC will contain the lighter.

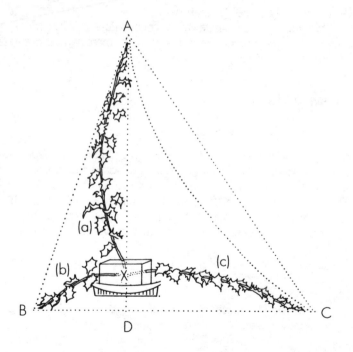

4   Use larger leaves to cover the mechanics. Use them particularly in the narrower triangle ABD to give weight and strength to that side of the design. Use smaller leaves in the wider triangle ADC.

All stems should appear to come from point X. Graduate the size of plant material carefully so that the design is a harmonious whole and does not have an arm sticking out.

5 Reinforce the outline with line flowers. Do not merely place them close to the limits but take them through the design.

6 Use focal flowers to create your area of greatest interest. This is always around the base of the tallest stem. It will therefore be off-centre. The balance will be asymmetrical.

7 Use filler material to complete the design. Do not worry if a small amount of foam is showing. If necessary cut your filler material very short and use it to cover the gaps. What you must not do is fill in your *scoop*. Create depth and interest without destroying your shape by angling some material backwards, particularly in the deepest part of your scoop.

8 Place your completed arrangement on an oval base. This will add to the visual stability.

The asymmetrical triangle arrangement

7
— UPRIGHT CIRCULAR —
ARRANGEMENT

This circular arrangement is seen to best effect when there is an abundance of plant material available. It has a loose, uncontrived feel and seems artlessly simple. It must have a raised container as the extra height is needed to complete your circle. This is a symmetrical design, where each side of the central axis will be similar but not the same. It is therefore best placed centrally, perhaps on a hall table or chest.

Components

The components are as follows:

- A raised container at least 25 cm high.
- A large candlecup and fix if a candlestick is being used. If you feel your candlecup is not going to be large enough to take all your plant material, use a vase which is not too heavy or one of the containers specially made for flower arranging available from flower club sales tables and some garden centres.
- Some foam. As a large amount of plant material is to be used the foam needs to be very firmly secured to the container with a frog and fix and/or tape.
- Curved line material and straight line material.
- Line flowers.
- Concealer leaves. As this is usually quite a large design these leaves also need to be large. Fatshedera, bergenia, hosta and large ivy leaves are good examples.
- Focal flowers.
- Filler material.

Method

1   Stem (*a*) of straight plant material should be the height of the container plus the height of the foam, which should rise 3–5 cm above the rim of the container. It is placed in the centre of the foam slightly towards the back. The line YZ is the diameter of your circle. Your other placements will all be placed to fill in this circle. The base of your container (Z) is completing the circle. X is not only the imaginary point from which all stems should radiate, it is also the central point of the circle.

2   Stems (*b*) are the same length as (*a*). Ideally these should have a slight curve. As in the symmetrical triangle, they are placed in each side of the foam, towards the top, angled downwards. You have now placed the basic spokes of your circle.

3   Two placements (*c*) at the front and two placements (*c*) at the back of your arrangement are all three quarters the length of placements (*a*) and (*b*). These are inserted in the sides of the foam angled downwards. Ideally these should also be slightly curved.

4   Placements (*d*), the same length as (*a*) and (*b*), are inserted in the top of the foam. All stems must appear to radiate outwards from

Line material: escallonia, sorrel, delphinium, griselinia and rosemary

Concealer material, clockwise from top: hosta, bergenia, fatshedera, heuchera ('Palace Purple'), tellima, *Alchemilla mollis* and, centre, tolmeia

Focal material, clockwise from top left: dahlia, lily, gerbera, scabious and rudbeckia

Filler material, clockwise from top: pittosporum, skimmia, euonymus, *Viburnum tinus* and alstroemeria

The round table arrangement with privet, geranium leaves, daisy chrysanthemums and *Alchemilla mollis*

The horizontal table arrangement with ivy, flowering currant, roses and *Viburnum tinus*

The downward crescent with honeysuckle, heuchera, roses and sorrel

The symmetrical triangle arrangement using complementary colours –
yellow and purple

The asymmetrical triangle arrangement using flowers of adjacent colours

An upward crescent arrangement with curving pussy willow

Mimosa creates the outline of this Hogarth Curve design

The diagonal arrangement: basket and plant material complement each other in form and outline

Flowers in a vase: the soft tints of the flowers harmonise well with eucalyptus

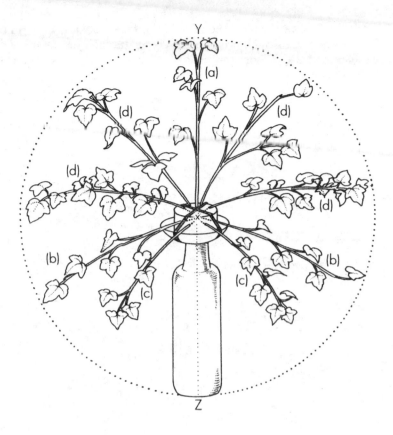

the imaginary point X at the centre of the foam. The tips of these stems must touch the boundary of the imaginary dotted line circle or fall short. They must not go beyond it. Depending on the size of your arrangement and the width of your line material you will need between 6–10 stems. Angle two or three stems backwards to build up depth and therefore interest.

5 Ensure that you have spokes at regular intervals through the design.

6 Place concealer leaves through the design. Do not concentrate these leaves too close to the foam. Use some on longer stems through the design to graduate the heaviness through to the lighter tips.

7 Add line flowers to take the colour almost to the circle boundaries and to fill in any wide gaps between the outline material.

8 Add focal flowers around the base of the tallest stem (*a*).

9 Add filler foliage and flowers. Take colour through the design and round the back. Fill out the circle so that the design looks full and abundant.

The upright circular arrangement

8

—— THE UPWARD —— CRESCENT

The upward crescent is a stylised but effective design. It uses only a small amount of plant material. Unlike the downward crescent – which has sides of approximately the same length – the upward crescent looks better when one side is longer than the other, as in the drawing on the right. Both sides being equal can give the impression of bulls' horns as in the drawing on the left. It is usual to follow a generous curve of the new moon.

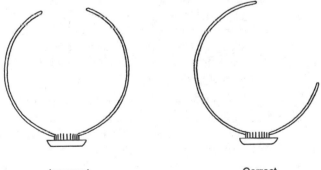

Incorrect   Correct

This design cannot be created without curved line material. If you cannot find any, do not attempt it. However, some plant material can be encouraged to curve. Broom can be soaked for a couple of hours and then tied in the required shape. When dried it will be permanently curved but make sure you do not overdo it or else you will find you have created a circle. Blossom is ideal as it takes colour and flowers to the tips of the design without the addition of extra stems which can muddy the outline. Japonica (quince) often has lovely curves and in the spring looks stunning in this design. Flexible plant material such as willow or dogwood can be encouraged to bend using warm hands.

The plant material needs to be kept firmly in place and although you can use foam, a pinholder is recommended. If stems are not carefully placed in foam they can swing round. A pinholder can easily be covered either with plant material, moss or small pebbles. Covering foam can lead to a fussy effect that destroys the clarity of the desired shape.

Plant material with hard stems should have its stem ends cut at a sharp angle before being eased between or onto the pins. It can then be angled by gentle pressure. Be careful when placing hard material as the pins are sharp. If a stem refuses to stay in place – and this can happen to even the most accomplished of arrangers – slit the stem upwards. It will then go on the pins more easily and you will not damage the holder. However, slitting stems is not recommended generally (see page 19). Softer stems should be placed onto the pins. Thin stems are difficult to use on a pinholder. A way of overcoming this is to tie several stems together with wool or adhesive tape and try again.

Make sure that the pinholder is firmly secured to your chosen container with a 'sausage' of fix round the circumference or three pieces placed at regular intervals. The Japanese keep pinholders in place by balance alone as an unfixed pinholder can be repositioned in the container at will. If you wish to do this, place the pinholder on a thin square of polystyrene wrapping or damp newspaper while you create your arrangement, as this will prevent the pinholder from sliding across a shiny surface or scratching it.

The pinholder can then either be placed in a low shallow bowl (such as an earthenware dish) or in a small container on a base. A base is needed in the latter instance to balance the shape of the design. A low dish is used so that the viewer can look down on the design.

Balance in flower arranging should be both visual and actual. Actual balance means the design does not fall over. Visual balance means our eye feels comfortable and we do not worry that with one puff it will fall over.

The design on the left looks top heavy. The addition of a base on the right stabilises the design. Good balance has been achieved.

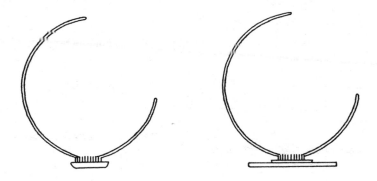

In flower arranging the plant material should always be more important than the container. This can be achieved by the plant material being 1½–2 times taller than the width of a low container. The upper limit is used if the line material is light and airy and the lower limit if heavy and strong. If the container is small, as in the drawings above, the design should be 1½–2 times taller than the width of the base, not just the container.

Components

The components are as follows:

- A pinholder with a 6.25 cm (2.5") diameter is usually the best size to start with.
- Some fix.
- A small container just large enough to take the pinholder and which allows the pins to be covered by water, plus a base. Alternatively use a large oval dish.
- Some flat pebbles or moss to hide the pinholder (optional).
- Curved line material such as broom, rosemary, blossom, pussy willow, forsythia.
- Line flowers with curved stems (if you are using blossom this may not be necessary). Spray carnations can be pruned to form a curve.
- Concealer leaves.
- Focal flowers.
- Filler material (little will be needed).

Method

1 Place a stem of curved plant material in the pinholder (*a*). The tip can come over the centre of the pinholder but not beyond it. This piece should be twice the length of the shallow dish. If a small container and a base are being used the first stem should be twice the length of the base. This is the upper height limit as only a small amount of plant material is being used.

2 The second stem of curved material (*b*) should be half to two thirds the length of (*a*) and should be placed so that the imaginary dotted line shown in the diagram would approximately complete the circle.

3 If blossom or other full material is being used as line placements, then (*c*) may not be necessary. If you are using fine pieces reinforce with shorter pieces (*c*).

4 Use concealer leaves with perhaps a few small stones to cover your pinholder. Always bear in mind the clean-cut sickle effect you are creating.

5 Line flowers can reinforce the shape, but do not try to do the impossible with stems that are too rigid, such as iris, or with buds that will open later to spoil your outline. Also, keep your colour scheme reasonably simple. If for example yellow is used for your focal

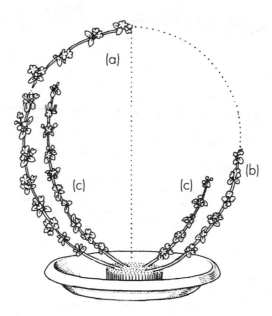

flowers make sure that the colour is extended through your design, perhaps using yellow spray carnations as line material.

6 Create the focal area. This should be in the area at the base of the tallest stem. If stem (*a*) does not come over as far as the centre of the pinholder, your focal area may be slightly off-centre. Only use one or two focal flowers at this point. If possible place a few smaller flowers and their buds further into the curve to link the outer parts of the design with the centre so that the design is a harmonious whole.

7 If necessary complete the shape with filler material. This is not always required.

8 Look at your design and remove any pieces of plant material which are superfluous. Check that you do not have an accumulation of leaves at the base which will spoil the smooth line of the curve. Space and a clear-cut outline are very important. Less really is more in this design. Cover any mechanics which still show with moss or flat pebbles rather than with more plant material.

The upward crescent arrangement

Try another crescent shape, perhaps with the tip of the tallest stem stopping well short of the dotted line. Your focal area will still be in the area at the base of the tallest stem but this will now be off-centre.

9
— HOGARTH —
CURVE

The Hogarth curve is attributed to the famous artist of the same name who called it the *Line of Beauty*. It loosely follows the shape of the letter S. It is a stylised shape but it gives the arranger a keen sense of achievement. The successful Hogarth curve means that the arranger understands his/her material and is able to display his/her knowledge to stunning effect.

The tall thin shape means it is ideal for narrow alcoves or where space is at a premium. Its economy of plant material means that impact does not necessarily have to be expensive.

Do not attempt this design unless you have curved plant material and a tall raised container.

Components

The components are as follows:

- A tall raised container at least 25 cm high. If a bottle or candlestick is being used, a small candlecup will be needed.
- A small amount of foam. It must not fill the candlecup as the more foam used, the more plant material will be needed. This can detract from the smoothness of your shape. It must however rise well above the rim.
- Curved line material. This is essential. Blossom is ideal as it takes the colour through to the limits of the design.
- Concealer leaves.
- Focal flowers.
- Filler material.

Method

1   The first placement (*a*) must be curved plant material. It should be about one and a half times the height of your container and placed in the middle of the foam two thirds of the way back. It should be upright or angled very slightly backwards. It must not lean forwards. The tip of this stem must have an imaginary line to the centre of your foam. It must not cross over it. This will not work unless the plant material has a strong curve as in the diagram opposite.

2   The second stem of curved material (*b*) is approximately one third to one half the length of (*a*). It is positioned to come forward towards the viewer. It should appear to be a natural extension of (*a*). The stem end is inserted in the side of the foam, or the front, so that it comes forward to create, together with placement (*a*), an informal S shape. The tip of stem (*b*) should form a vertical line with the tip of stem (*a*). This would give the dotted line YZ on the diagram opposite. Each stem therefore must appear to come from the imaginary X as in the other designs.

3   Place concealer leaves to cover some of the oasis. Take great care not to detract from your S shape.

4   Line flowers may be added to reinforce the foliage line and to take colour through. Ensure that they are shorter than the foliage and that they follow the shape.

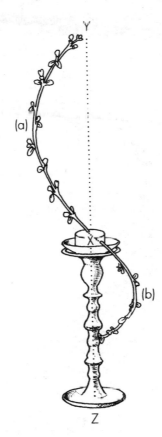

5 Place a focal flower at the base of your tallest stem (*a*). Other focal flowers can be used to graduate the shape carefully towards the extremities but these should be smaller or angled so that they are less dominant. Remember that one flower of a different variety or colour stands out too vividly and stops the design being seen as a whole.

6 Cover any foam still showing with short pieces of filler. Use the minimum amount of material possible. Do remember that you will be far more conscious of foam showing than anyone else. It is better to have space in your design and be able to see the form of all your components than have it overfilled.

Fill out the shape. Think of the overall shape with every placement made. Do not use any material that is going to obscure the shape of the S in any way. You will now be thankful that you used the minimum amount of foam.

The Hogarth curve

10
—— THE DIAGONAL ——

Boxes or baskets with lids are ideal containers for a diagonal design using few flowers to stunning effect. A shallow container is placed in the box or basket and your foam placed within it. It is essential that the foam rises well above the rim of the box.

The lid of your box must obviously be kept open by some means. This is easily done by wedging a strong piece of stem under each side of the lid. These can be removed to make the arranging easier, inserted again on completion and adjusted if necessary.

Components

The components are as follows:

- A rectangular box or basket with a lid. A round container does not look nearly as effective with a diagonal arrangement.
- A small inner container.
- Sufficient foam to rise well above the rim of the box or basket.
- Straight line material. If your box is solid with deep sides use bolder line material, e.g. camellia. If you have a fine basketry box with shallow sides use finer, more delicate material such as ceanothus, kerria, forsythia or berberis.
- Concealer leaves.
- Focal flowers.
- Filler material.

Method

1   Place the foam and the inner container centrally in the box. Remember: the more foam you use the more you will have to cover. Only fill about one third of the area of the inside of the box with foam. It should rise between 2.5 cm and 7 cm above the rim of the container depending on the size of the box. Place strong pieces of stem to wedge the lid about three quarters open.

2   Place stem (*a*) out of the short side of the foam angled upwards. This stem should extend half the length of the box beyond the edge. If the length of your box is 30 cm, stem (*a*) should extend 15 cm beyond the edge. If the box is 20 cm long, the stem should extend 10 cm beyond the edge.

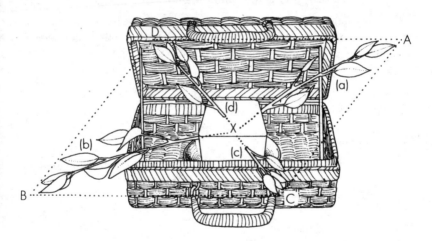

3   Stem (*b*) must appear as a continuation of stem (*a*). It should extend the same distance as stem (*a*) beyond the edge. This forms the diagonal AB.

4   Stem (*c*) is placed at a right angle to line AB. It should be angled downwards out of the foam so that it extends just over the rim.

5   Stem (*d*) is placed backwards at right angles to AB. You have now completed the diamond shape ACBD.

6   Use concealer leaves to cover some of the foam.

7 Place line flowers to reinforce line foliage and to take the colour almost to the limits. Take the flowers through the design to give unity.

8 Focal flowers should be placed centrally and graduated out following the line AB.

9 Add filler material. Little will be needed.

The diagonal arrangement

11
—— ELONGATED ——
TRIANGLE (VERTICAL)

The elongated triangle is quickly and easily created using three or five stems. Bulb flowers are often used for this design. Five iris or three stems of lilies are ideal. With practice this design will take you less than five minutes.

Components

The components are as follows:

- A wide shallow oval or round bowl. It could be a pyrex lid, or a small flan dish.
- A pinholder and fix.
- Five stems of iris or three stems of lilies. The method below is for five stems but is easily adapted for three. In the ideal world the five flowers in your bunch will have flowers at different stages of development: one bud, one more developed, one nearly full out and the rest in between. It is rarely the ideal world however so do not worry if all your flowers look exactly the same. Your design will still work. Iris can be encouraged to open by blowing gently into the bud.
- Three large round or oval leaves, such as fatsia, large ivy leaves, fatshedera, bergenia or hosta. Three aspidistra or tulip leaves can be used. Curve each leaf over and gently poke the sharp tip through the leaf at a point about three quarters of the way down. This will, or should, stay in place and you will have created enclosed space.
- Stones, pebbles, shells, marbles or moss to cover the mechanics.

Method

1 Fix the pinholder centrally in the container.
2 The first flower stem (*a*) should be about two and a half times the length of the container. This should be the tightest bud. It is placed centrally, towards the back of the pinholder, angled very slightly backwards.
3 The second stem (*b*) is three quarters the length of (*a*). This is placed to one side of the first stem (*a*). It should be upright and not angled backwards. If possible this should be a fuller bud than (*a*).
4 Stem (*c*) is three quarters the length of (*b*). It is placed upright to the other side of (*a*).
5 The fourth stem (*d*) is three quarters the length of (*c*). It is placed approximately in front of, or slightly to the inside of (*b*). It is angled slightly forwards.

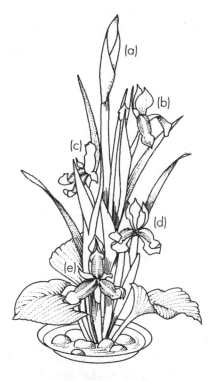

The elongated triangle arrangement

6 The fifth stem (*e*) is three quarters the length of stem (*d*). This will be a short stem. It is placed close to the base, between stems (*a*) and (*c*). This should be your most fully-opened flower and also placed coming slightly forward.

7 Three large leaves or three looped leaves should be placed on the pinholder. Angle them and have them on different lengths of stem to avoid a static, frilly effect. These leaves will form the elongated triangle with the tip of stem (*a*).

8 Cover the pinholder with your pebbles, shells or marbles.

9 Do try this design with other flowers.

12

── LANDSCAPE ── DESIGN

For a landscape design the arranger's objective is to recreate a scene from nature. The landscape design calls for arrangers to use their eyes rather than their money. Observation and a few snippets from the countryside will create a long lasting design greatly enjoyed by lovers of nature.

Different landscapes can be created according to the habitat you have visited and/or wish to depict. A hedgerow landscape could include bark, moss, ferns and a plant of yellow primulas (representing the quickly diminishing population of the native primrose which must never be uprooted and preferably not picked). A lakeland scene might contain bullrushes, flag iris and pebbles while a seascape might be created from thistles, driftwood, seaweed, thrift or shells.

It should become obvious that florists' flowers such as carnations are not in context. The feeling should be of nature and not of the greenhouse.

The simplest form of landscape design uses an interesting branch to give height. It can be bare or in leaf. This represents a tree. It should be inserted into foam or onto a pinholder within a container which can be easily concealed. Bark, pebbles and/or small pieces of wood are excellent for concealing. Pet shops often sell exciting pieces of wood for aquariums which are perfect for this design. Place the branch off-centre to create a more informal asymmetrical shape.

As the various parts to this design need to be unified it is highly advisable to use a base which will pull all these components together: perhaps slate for a lakeland scene, a slice of wood for a woodland scene or a sheet of sandpaper for a seascape. Do not use finest velvet on a smooth round base. Nature's shapes are much more irregular.

Landscape design

Once your 'tree' is in place your imagination can take over. Observe the world you are wanting to depict – take a closer look at the hedgerow and its wealth of different plant material. Explore the sand dunes. Observe the moss, the ferns, the lichens, the cottonflowers on the moor and take that memory home to recreate the image there.

If you desire further guidelines the information below may help.

- If using accessories – that is anything other than plant material, such as stones or shells – do not scatter them all over your base. Group them.

- Use less material rather than more. Do not cram too much material into a small area. Allow space in your design. This landscape is representing your scene in microcosm. Your effect will be all the greater if the items you are using can be seen individually and are not blurring one into the other.

- Manmade accessories do not work as well as those from nature. China animals are charming as ornaments but if they are shiny they will not fit into your scene. Those with a dull rough texture may.

- Try to have all parts of your landscape 'in scale'. Remember that your branch is your tree, so if you were to use a figurine as an accessory it would have to be of a size which would be in harmony with your 'tree'.

- As the landscape design is often understated, much can be made of the subtlety of different textures. You could have the smoothness of pebbles beaten by the waves, the sharpness of coral, the softness of moss, the roughness of bark. Different textures enhance each other by their contrasts but, just as you need the plain concealer leaves to throw up the beauty of busier material, the calmer surfaces seen in pebbles or an expanse of still water against the prickly texture of, say, teasles, increases awareness of the characteristics of both.

Legally the landowner's permission should be sought before taking any plant material from the countryside. However it is generally acceptable to take material where it grows in profusion provided that only small amounts are taken. Under no account should plants be picked unless they can be identified as common and widespread. Plants should never be uprooted. Allow the leaves of snowdrops or bluebells to remain so that food can go back into the bulb for the following year.

13
——— COLOUR ———

The choice of colour is very personal and will remain so however much you read about others' use of it. What this book can do is provide you with a few guidelines which will help you to use colour more effectively by taking into consideration colour schemes, positioning and lighting.

There are only three colours – red, yellow and blue – which are not a mixture of other colours. These are called *primary colours* and it is these three combined together in different quantities which create all other colours. Mixing these primary colours in equal amounts produces secondary colours. Red and yellow produce orange. Yellow and blue produce green. Blue and red make violet. Orange, green and violet are called *secondary colours*.

——— The colour wheel ———

If the primary and secondary colours are arranged in a circle you have formed a colour wheel.

Red, yellow, blue, green, orange and violet are strong pure colours and if used in this strength can create a design which is stimulating and vibrant but tiring on the eye. Think of putting the colours of nasturtiums, cornflowers, daffodils, purple lilac and birds of paradise in one design. It certainly would not be a design for calm contemplation. If you are not in the mood to be over-stimulated and you are given a 'garage bunch', each flower with a different colour of full strength – perhaps a yellow dahlia, a red chrysanthemum, an orange spray carnation, and a purple aster all enveloped with tired gypsophila – do not despair. Green is the flower arranger's neutral colour and can be used a3 a restful foil for other colours. Cut the stems of your garage bunch short and add them to a basket or table centrepiece full of calm plain green foliage.

——— Tints, tones and shades ———

A pastel or *tint* is created when white is added to any strong pure colour which is therefore made lighter. A tint of orange is peach, a tint of yellow is cream and a tint of red is pink. The more white that is added the more the colour will become a barely tinted white. Tinted whites will give a lift and sparkle to any colour combination that you are considering. Think of cream cow parsley added to alstroemeria, *Viburnum tinus* added to spray chrysanthemums and cream or pale yellow variegated foliage within a table arrangement of red carnations and dark green holly.

Tints are generally easy to combine and give a light happy effect. Be careful about placing pastel flowers in the bright light of a window as this will dim their beauty.

Conversely, *shades* are created when black is added to the pure colour which then becomes darker. Examples are brown, gold and maroon. An arrangement consisting only of shades can look rather dismal. They need the addition of tints to bring them to life.

So tints or pastels are made when white is added to the pure colour, shades if black is added. *Tones* are created when grey is added. Tones subdue pure colour. Good examples of tones can often be seen in dried flower arrangements. Toned colours are soft and usually pleasing to the eye.

——— Monochromatic colours ———

A monochromatic colour scheme is one that uses tints, tones and shades of one colour. This colour scheme can be used effectively in a room with strongly patterned wallpaper. Interest in the arrangement can be heightened by the use of strong textural contrasts.

Adjacent colours

Colours lying next to each other on the colour wheel, together with their tints, tones and shades are called *adjacent colours*. They give easy pleasing colour schemes. Many flower shops now colour block their selection into reds, blues and yellows, together with their adjacent colours. This can help you in your choice of flowers.

Complementary colours

If colours on opposite sides of the rainbow wheel are used together, such as red and green or yellow and purple, then a more dynamic colour scheme is achieved. Any two complementary colours used together intensify and so enhance each other brilliantly. Put blue flowers against an orange background and observe the clarity with which you perceive the flowers. Nature produces many examples of complementary harmonies such as purple pansies with yellow centres, the orange and blue of strelitzias and the red and green of tulips.

Generally speaking, blues and greens show up best against a white background – think of blue clematis growing up a whitewashed wall – and reds and yellows are enhanced by a dark background. Think of geraniums or yellow-leaved ivy against a dark wooden fence.

If you do enjoy strong pure colour do not use equal amounts of two colours, particularly if they are complementary. Let one colour dominate so that the two colours do not vie and pull the eye in different directions causing discordance. However, do not use just one flower of a particular colour. A single yellow flower in a design of other colours will stick out like a sore thumb. The eye will home in on the one yellow flower and be unable to travel round and enjoy the rest of the arrangement. If other yellow flowers are scattered through the eye will move round and enjoy all dimensions of the design. This eye movement is called *rhythm* in flower-arranging parlance.

Warm and cool colours

Blues and greens and their tints and tones are cool colours. They make you feel cool because of their association with leaves, water, sea and sky. Reds and oranges are warm colours. They are the colours which are nearest to the colour of the sun. Yellow can be warm or cool depending on whether it is with warm or cool colours. Warm and cool therefore refer to the effect that these colours have on your senses. If the day is cool or the room is north-facing with little direct sunshine then you will feel warm too if you fill it with warm colours. If it is mid-summer and the room faces directly south, feel the cooling effect of the blues and greens in your arrangement. The aspect of your room can also help you to decide on your colour scheme for the room. The use of complementary colours links a warm colour with a cool one.

Setting

Although it is satisfying to create an arrangement which reflects the overall décor of the room, it is also enjoyable to complement ornaments or perhaps a special feature at closer quarters. Picking out one or more of the colours in your 'accessory' can train your eye to try out exciting combinations of colour which you might never have considered. Shells for example contain myriad wonderful colours. Closer examination of natural objects always reveals more than would ever have been imagined.

If your design is for a buffet or dinner party ensure that the colour of the china or table napkins is echoed in the flowers. Within the arrangement itself colour harmony is essential. Flowers, container, base and candle if used should all be linked by colour. Never put a blue candle in a pink and green arrangement without adding, for example, blue cornflowers. Do not use a yellow base for a red and blue arrangement.

Colour movement

An interesting phenomenon is that some colours advance – they appear to reach out towards you – and others recede – they seem to vanish into the background. This can be observed in all manner of things. British Rail have some amazing striped seat covers. On one example which has black, red, mid-blue and orange stripes, you will be more aware of the orange, then the red, then the blue and finally the black. This is because orange advances and black recedes. Idle the time away on your next journey and analyse the seat covers. Of all the colours of the rainbow, yellow advances the most, then orange. Green follows, then red and lastly the blues and purples. Any colour which has white added to the pure colour will also advance further, whereas the addition of black will do the reverse.

In flower arranging the advancing and receding of colours is most important when arranging flowers in a large room, perhaps a hall or church. At a distance pastel colours will come towards you and stand out, giving you the effect you want. Dark flowers (particularly blue) recede into nothingness and can appear as holes. They will not be noticeable either in shape, texture or colour. Therefore they are a bad investment (holes look cheap!) so keep to lighter colours for larger arrangements. Be careful with the use of white flowers. They can look like blobs unless placed with pastel rather than dark coloured flowers.

Balance

Colour is an effective way of achieving balance. Pastel colours appear lighter in weight than darker colours or those which are strong and bright. Therefore place darker colours low and central and lighter colours closer to the edges. Be careful using white at the limits of a design which is predominantly of stronger or darker colours as white is extremely eye-catching and your balance may be upset.

Lighting

Lighting alters colour. The subtle light of candles gently shows up the pastel colours. Darker colours disappear. Fluorescent light brings blue and violet flowers to life but muddies reds and oranges. Electric tungsten lighting (household lighting) has the opposite effect. Reds and oranges are enhanced but blues are deadened. So think of the effect of lighting when choosing your colours.

Colour is evocative of a thousand emotions. It spurs creativity. It sets the scene. Experiment with colour. Combinations which seem impossible will work when flowers are the medium.

14
—— HOUSEPLANTS WITH ——
FLOWERS
(POT-ET-FLEUR)

A *pot-et-fleur* is the most amazingly long-lasting creation. It is often read about unenthusiastically but if created is viewed as one of the wonders of the flower-arranging world. A *pot-et-fleur* is an arrangement of growing plants grouped together in one container with additional cut flowers. The great advantage is that with careful choice you have a variety of plants in close proximity which give an instant luxuriant foliage background to a few flowers. With care the pot plants will last for years and you will only need to change the cut flowers according to whim, gift or the season. The *pot-et-fleur* could be termed the instant flower arrangement. The format could not be simpler. It is a boon for the busy arranger.

Components

You will need a container large enough and deep enough to take at least three plants. The size will depend on the space you have available for your container and the size and number of plants you wish to use. For suitable plants first look at those you have in the home – perhaps only one or two, but this is a good start. Many varieties will look and feel happier placed together. If they are easy to care for, so much the better.

You will need one tall plant. There are many easy pot plants which give height, such as aspidistra, fatshedera, *Grevillea robusta* (silk oak), ivy, sentry palm, philodendron, grape ivy or sansevieria. You will also need at least one trailing plant such as one of the asparagus ferns, a spider plant, a trailing ivy, a tradescantia or perhaps a peperomia. If the plants you have chosen are fussy or have a strong variegation, choose a filler plant which is calm and plain as your third plant. Conversely if the plants used are unexciting add zing with an aluminium, maranta or euonymus plant which has variegation or interesting markings. As long as you have one each of these three types of plant you can add any others to fill the space available. You will need about one and a half to two times the volume of flowers and foliage to the volume of your container. Do not worry too much about plant names. Just go to your florist or garden centre and choose the right shapes.

The plants you have chosen can be used either in or out of their own containers. It takes a little more time initially to prepare your large container to take plants without individual containers. But it is worth the effort for they take up much less space and overall prove less work.

Method

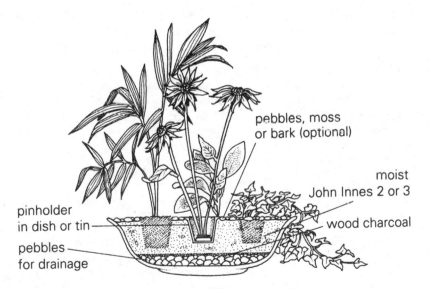

pebbles, moss or bark (optional)

moist John Innes 2 or 3

pinholder in dish or tin

wood charcoal

pebbles for drainage

Your container could be a Victorian wash bowl, a large basket, which would have to be lined with thick polythene or a piece of a dustbin bag, or a cooking bowl. The bottom of this container should have a layer of pebbles for drainage. However pebbles can scratch, so if you wish to preserve your container an excellent substitute can be made from the polystyrene plant trays that most garden centres love to give away. When broken into small pieces they make an ideal drainage material. Put in just sufficient to cover the bottom of your container. A thin layer of wood charcoal should be scattered on top. This is not the sort you put on barbecues. It is almost a powder and comes in small boxes from garden centres. This will keep your *pot-et-fleur* smelling sweet. Next add your compost. Avoid garden soil whatever the temptation. It should be John Innes number 2 or the equivalent. John Innes is not a brand name but a formula. In this sterile compost your plants will thrive. Add a thin layer before removing your pot plants from their containers and adding them to the large bowl.

Place your tall plant towards the back. Allow your trailing plant to fall over the front of your container. It may be positioned at an angle if you wish. Fill in with your other plants. You will need to leave a space for the inclusion of a pinholder or a piece of wet foam placed in a tin, a small jam jar or yoghurt pot. This space can be anywhere but is most usually central in the design. Your flowers can now be added. Bold shapes have most effect: you could use three gerberas, a few garden roses, five iris in the spring or rudbeckia in the autumn.

Group the stems close together at different heights but none taller than the outline created by your foliage plants. Add more compost if needed. A layer of moss may be placed on top of the soil if so desired or use a few flat pebbles to give interest. You could insert a branch or a piece of driftwood into your pinholder or compost if you felt that your design lacked height. When your flowers are past their best replace them with a few more fresh flowers.

You can keep the leaves of your pot plants in good order by wiping off the dust with greaseproof paper. This will give them a healthy shine. Add plant food when appropriate.

You can make other designs with houseplants. One large bushy houseplant can give an exotic long-lasting arrangement in seconds. A Boston fern or grape ivy works brilliantly. Simply buy two or three stems of Singapore orchids, which are not as expensive as you might think and are usually sold with their own individual water vials. Support these in the soil and arrange your orchids through the leaves. If the plant is tall and heavy you could hide a couple of the vials high up amongst the leaves. If you have a hanging basket in your home, allow them to trail down.

A hanging basket with orchids

Today paper and silk flowers are extremely realistic. Add one or two to your pot plants. Make sure the flowers are in scale. Only use one type per plant, use flowers in season – say roses in summer – and try to link the foliage to the accompanying flowers in size and form. A carnation and an iris in an aspidistra plant, or daffodils with an African violet, are going to fool no one!

15
— FLOWERS —
IN A VASE

Flowers placed simply in a vase can look stunning. They can also look dreadful. However there are some basic guidelines for the selection of the vase, the use of mechanics and the choice of flowers which will make your designs work to happy effect.

—————— The vase ——————

If you are planning to buy or borrow a vase, and a vase here means any container which is taller than it is wide, consider the following:

- Avoid those vases with a narrow opening in relation to their width (*a*), or those which are too wide in relation to their base (*b*). These

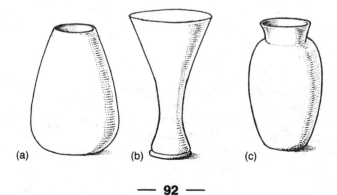

(a)   (b)   (c)

latter vases can only be used effectively if a base is added to give visual stability. Wedding present vases are sometimes best left as ornaments. Vase *(c)* provides better balance.

- Vases that have a very strong pattern or a shiny texture will overpower most flowers. White containers are very dominant, particularly if they are shiny as well. However, white flowers alone in a white vase or with the addition of green or cream-variegated foliage or pastel flowers can give a stunning effect. If the colours of your flowers are mixed, try to include some white flowers.

- If you like the shape and size of your vase or it is the only one at your disposal but the colours are awful, take a piece of fabric – perhaps a plain piece or even a patterned one which matches your room. Stand your vase on the material and lift it so that it totally covers the vase. Tie the fabric near the top with cord, braid or raffia and tuck the ragged edges in.

- Vases which have an incurving lip are not easy. Downward flow and thus a graceful natural design is much more difficult to achieve.

- The heavier the container, and of course visually pottery looks heavier than glass, the more material you will need for good proportions. If a pottery or stoneware vase is shaped then it is lighter visually.

- Vases in the shallow, elongated style of the 1950s are tricky. They need care, time and an experienced arranger if they are to be made to look effective. Because of their shape they need a lot of plant material. Look at the volume in the drawing below.

- The inside of glass, plastic or ceramic vases, which can be thoroughly cleaned, will keep flowers longer in good health. Copper, brass and silver containers are lovely but cannot be cleaned as easily. If you want to use a copper or silver container then place another container, such as a glass coffee jar, inside.

The mechanics

The mechanics you use will depend on the vase you use. Wire netting is often used in pottery, stone or plastic – in fact in any vase where it will not show and will not cause damage by scratching. It can be purchased from ironmongers or DIY stores in different mesh sizes. A good-sized mesh for using as a mechanic inside vases is the 50 mm. Green plastic netting is sold in many garden centres especially for flower arranging. The advantages are that it does not scratch delicate materials and it will not rust. It is however more expensive. In the past it has not been considered as pliable as garden netting but new techniques now mean this is no longer necessarily true.

The amount you use depends to some extent on the size of the container and the thickness of the stems you wish to insert. A rough guideline would be to cut a piece a little wider than the width of the opening and about three times the depth. Cut off the selvedge as this is stiff. Crumple the netting so that it forms approximately the same shape as the container. Try if possible to keep some loose ends at the top so that they can be twisted round thick stems to give added support.

If you need extra support, particularly if you are using thick-stemmed heavy branches, place a pinholder in the bottom of your vase. Let your first placement through the wire netting be well impaled on the pinholder and this will firmly secure the netting, as shown opposite.

If your stems are short and your container is deep, use sand as your mechanics. Pour it into your vase to the required depth, add water and then your stems. A pinholder can be placed on the sand to give extra support if so desired.

Glass containers obviously call for different mechanics. Wire netting through glass is not desirable. In this case use thin, transparent adhesive tape criss-crossed over the opening to give support. Once you have placed the plant material, the tape can be covered with bun or reindeer moss.

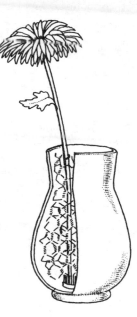

Wire netting in a vase

Marbles are visually noticeable mechanics which can add to a design in a glass vase. They can be expensive so look through the toy boxes before purchasing. It is a good idea to place a layer in your container, then arrange your stems and then add more marbles. If they are all in place before you start arranging, it can be difficult to wriggle your stems through.

Washed, round pebbles from the beach are cheaper and look just as effective. Try shells, plastic ice cubes or even bamboo stems cut and arranged within the glass vase before you start. Clear cellophane can be scrunched up and placed in your glass vase.

Crystals that form a gel by the addition of water have long been used to limit the need for essential watering of tubs and hanging baskets. The gel can be used to good effect in glass containers and it does help to keep stems in place.

Food colouring can be added to the water in glass vases to give a colour link with the flowers. A drop of blue perhaps if your arrangement is of cornflowers and larkspur. Yellow for sunflowers or rudbeckia.

——— The plant material ———

The most important points to know before you start arranging flowers in a vase are as follows:

- The plant material should be about one and a half to two times the height of the vase for good proportion – (*a*) below is incorrect.
- If the plant material is not tall enough, the volume of the flowers used can compensate for the lack of height as in (*c*) below. Therefore less height means more flowers. The volume of flowers used should be about one and a half to two times the volume of the mass of the container. Conversely you can compensate for having only a few stems by going higher, as in (b).

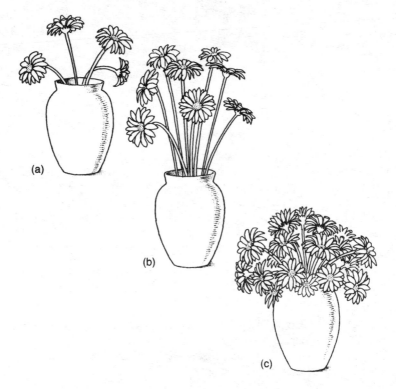

(a)

(b)

(c)

- Colour can compensate for lack of volume. Bright vivid colours and dark colours look visually heavier than pastel colours. They appear to weigh more. Therefore fewer vivid or dark flowers will be needed to offset the weight of the container than those of pastel colouring.

- Mixed colours of the same flower always look good. Mixed flowers succeed if there is close colour harmony, for example shades, tints and tones of adjacent colours.

- Flowers generally look their most effective if the harsh line of the rim of their container or vase is softened by the downward flow of the plant material. This can be achieved by:

  (a) Using plant material such as tulips which usually have a natural bend and will gracefully curve over the rim.

  (b) Using plant material such as peonies which have their own attractive foliage high up on the stem which can fall gently over the rim.

  (c) Adding leaves to the flowers which will curve over the rim, perhaps long-lasting aspidistra leaves, eucalyptus, curving sprays of ivy or leather fern which can be purchased from many florists.

  (d) Adding long-lasting bear grass which is now available in bunches from many florists. Although bear grass looks similar to tough long garden grass, it lasts for weeks in arrangements and, if added to just ten spray carnations, adds charm and distinction. It is easier to use if the rubber band is kept round the stems, thus creating a fountain.

- Massed flowers of one type in a vase always look good but there must be enough of them. One bunch of freesias without help can look lost. Five stems of spray carnations look terrible. Fifteen to twenty stems are needed for most average-sized vases. Alternatively you can mix the five stems with others which have interest all down the stem such as *Viburnum tinus, Choisya ternata*, cow parsley, *Alchemilla mollis* or grevillea.

- Short stemmy flowers like freesias look good with herbs. Try them with long stems of parsley and chop away at the parsley when it is required for cooking. Keeping it in water will keep it fresh and its form and fresh green colour enhances many flowers.

- Reflect the colour of your vase in the flowers used. Copper is good with pinks, peaches, mauves, apricots and reds. Brass suits yellows, oranges, greens and browns. Silver, alabaster and pewter are lovely with pinks, blues and greys.

- If your container is of delicate china or glass, sustain the effect by using delicate flowers such as freesias or sweet peas. The earthiness of pottery or stoneware suits stronger forms such as dahlias, berries or hydrangeas.

Stand-by material

There will be times when you have minimal material. Perhaps friends coming to dinner offer you five stems of spray carnations which when unwrapped look like knobbly sticks with blobs of colour at the tips. Perhaps there is no time to create a shape. Perhaps the frosts have destroyed your foliage or your money needs to be spent elsewhere. Then is the time to take advantage of your stand-by props to complete your arrangements. These could be any of the following:

Eucalyptus

Fresh eucalyptus can be picked and dried at any time of the year. Just pick or buy several stems and hang them upside down in a warm dry atmosphere. Five stems of dried eucalyptus, with its interest down the stem, gives instant volume and strength to a bunch of flowers.

Another way to preserve eucalyptus is to place the bottom 2.5 cm of stem in a solution of one part glycerine mixed well with two parts boiling water. Insert the stems when the liquid has cooled and leave in a dry place for two to three weeks, by which time the stem will have taken the glycerine solution up to the leaves and they will have become pliant and leathery. Eucalyptus treated in this way can even be washed in warm soapy water. This method can be used to preserve many kinds of foliage. However, deciduous foliage should only be preserved at the height of its season, for example beech in July before it prepares itself for leaf fall.

Hydrangeas

Hydrangeas are some of the most valuable of dried flowers. They can be added where volume is needed so they can be particularly useful when a large heavy container is to be used. If your stem ends become soggy, chop them off and use them in a shorter vase next time.

Dried hydrangeas are exorbitantly expensive to buy so if you do not have a bush, find one belonging to a good friend or neighbour who will be amenable to pruning. However, remember that hydrangeas only flower on the old wood so if you take all the flowers there will be none the following year. To dry the heads the stems should be cut in the autumn just before the onslaught of the heavy frosts. The heads should feel slightly papery to the touch. If they dry out too quickly the heads will shrivel, so place the stems in 5 cm of water. Do not replace this water. The heads will then dry out more slowly and shrivelling will be minimised.

Stems with lichen and larch branches

These can be stored indefinitely in boxes until needed. They give bulk and good textural interest to all flowers but are particularly effective with spring flowers.

A pot-et-fleur

A *pot-et-fleur* can provide the background for any flowers from daffodils to orchids. Have your pinholder or foam ready to add your flowers. Your friends will not see a mere *pot-el-fleur* with flowers added. They will see a glorious arrangement incorporating their floral gift.

Try these ideas and you should soon find that you can cope easily and effortlessly with any bunch of flowers which is presented to you.

16
— GIFTS OF FLOWERS —

Gifts have to be portable. When you know that the recipients will wish to arrange the flowers themselves, a cellophane wrap is ideal. Others cannot or will not be in a position to arrange them. Perhaps they are in hospital or having guests to dinner. On these occasions a ready-made design would be greatly appreciated. For those who know little about foam make sure that your gift, where appropriate, has a good supply of water. Remind your recipient to add water when necessary.

—— A basket of fresh flowers ——

A basket of flowers is ideal for many occasions. One of the greatest merits of the basket arrangement is that it is so portable. It can be given as a gift and can be moved from room to room. It is ideal to take to a friend in hospital as it can be easily transported home afterwards.

Basketry in all its shapes and forms has a natural affinity with flowers and foliage. Knowing a few simple facts makes it difficult to go wrong. First of all take care when you buy your basket. Choose one in which it will be easy to arrange flowers. With a little more experience you will be able to go on and arrange baskets in all shapes and sizes, but to start with it is best to buy a basket which is neither too small nor too large. Between 20 cm and 30 cm is ideal. Darker baskets are always easy to use. They harmonise with whatever plant material is to be used. Light bleached basketry is more eye-catching. It may therefore be in competition with your flowers but can look stunning with careful selection of the plant material.

Some baskets have a deep base and a short handle, similar to (a) below. Lovely though these are, they can be difficult to arrange flowers in. Try to find a basket which has plenty of space between the basket rim and the top of the handle, as in (b) and (c). Also ensure that the handle crosses the short sides of the basket and not the long.

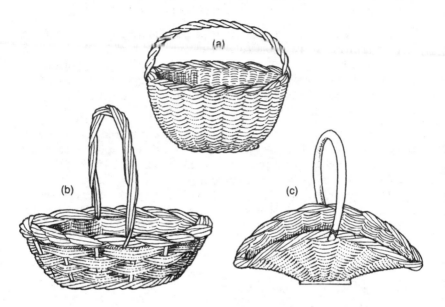

Some baskets now come ready lined. It is a good precaution to line an unlined basket and this is easily done. Take a piece of thick polythene. Dark dustbin liners will be fine for darker baskets and clear polythene for the lighter ones. Cut it to fit the inside of the basket and then sew with ordinary thread and needle around the rim of the basket.

If possible place a container inside the basket, though foam can be placed directly onto the polythene with the help of a frog. As with the other designs, the foam you use must come well above the rim of the basket. Do not be tempted to make it level with the rim. It is extremely important with a basket arrangement that there is a downward flow over the rim. Do not fill the entire inside with foam. Too much foam means too much material and, as a consequence, loss of space.

Choose plant material which is harmonious with your container. Think twice about a combination such as orchids and daffodils. If you are worried about combinations, you will always be safe mixing flowers which have been grown under the same conditions, e.g. all hothouse plants together, tropical plant material together and garden plants together.

Also think about scale. If your basket is small, use small flowers and if big, use big flowers. Large flower heads in a small basket fill it too easily and give a static, uninteresting effect.

It used to be popular to create an asymmetrical design in a basket but now it is much more usual to repeat the shape of the basket with flowers and foliage. A round basket should have a round arrangement. An oval basket should have an oval arrangement. Some shapes of basket defy any repetition, but avoid those until you have had a go at a more conventional design.

Most baskets have a handle and if there is one it should be allowed to show. Do not smother the handle area so that it disappears as in (*a*) below. A basket is meant to be picked up. Smothering the handle area usually means that your proportion of plant material to basket is too great. As a rough guide (*b*) there should be approximately one and a half to two times the volume of plant material to the volume of the basket.

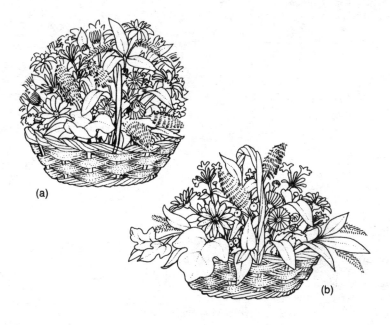

(a)

(b)

A tied bunch

A tied bunch is a bunch of flowers and foliage which has been arranged and tied firmly in the hand, ready to be placed in a vase without further preparation. Some florists will prepare one for you. But how much nicer to be able to add foliage from the garden or cow parsley from the hedgerow or riverbank to your own carefully selected flowers.

Components

You will need fifteen to twenty stems of flowers, with or without foliage attached. When you are selecting your plant material you should consider the following:

- Avoid flowers which are in tight bud because you will want immediate impact.
- Avoid flowers with soft stems such as daffodils and anemones because they may be squashed when they are being tied.
- Try to use some stems with a curve, or try flowing bear grass. This will soften your design.
- Choose flowers with approximately the same lifespan.
- When selecting it is often easiest to think in terms of colour but think also of form. (Form is something with depth and is therefore three-dimensional.) You will need your round focal flowers and line flowers. Together they will enhance each other. Choose one or more varieties with interest down the stem.
- Avoid stems which branch low down.
- Avoid stems which are very thick. Thin stems are easier to hold.
- Flowers with great variance in their stem length can be awkward to handle together.

You will also need some twine or ribbon. Best of all for keeping the stems firmly in place is a slim plastic electrician's tie which works on a ratchet mechanism. It provides a firm tie and does not cut into the stems. A bow can be placed over the tie to finish it off.

Method

1   Strip the leaves from the bottom half of the stems.
2   Have your twine or tie and scissors close to hand.

3 Place your hand so that the space between the thumb and first finger forms a narrow vase. You will relax your hand as more stems are added.

4 You must now build up a spiral of flowers. All the stems must be angled in the same direction round a central pivot. The method for this is as follows:

(a) Insert a central vertical stem.

(b) Place the second stem at a slight angle across the vertical stem.

(c) Place the third stem at a sharper angle to the second stem as in (*a*) below or alternatively place it behind so that the flowers appear to circle round in the same direction, as in (*b*) below.

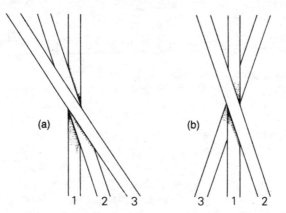

(d) Build up the spiral by placing all your stems one over the other or by placing one in front and then one behind, or a combination of both. What you must not do is to place one to the left of the central axis and then to the right and repeat. This method will *not* produce a spiral.

5 When all your stems have been included, tie your twine, raffia or string round and through the stems at the point at which they cross over each other. The electrician's tie just needs to be pulled firmly round the stems.

6 Trim the base of the stems to the same length. Add the bow and a wrap of cellophane if desired.

7 Do mention when presenting your tied bunch that the recipient should not untie it. He or she should simply recut the ends and place in water.

A tied bunch

Presentation wrap

A few flowers presented in a cellophane wrap can look as if they come from the best florist in town. This example uses three types of flowers. You may of course adapt these instructions to suit your taste and the plant material you have available.

Components

You will need the following:

- Clear or lightly patterned cellophane, about two and a half times the length of the tallest stem. This can be purchased from a large stationer's or from a good-natured florist.
- A tall stem of foliage such as laurel, camellia or privet. It needs to have a strong stem as this is going to be the backbone of your design.
- Some shorter pieces of foliage (optional).

- Five strong stems of tall flowers such as liatris, spray chrysan-themums, iris or spray carnations.
- Approximately five stems of round flowers, e.g. gerberas or car-nations.
- Approximately five more delicate, 'showy' flowers, such as roses or freesias.
- Twine or an electrician's tie.
- Ribbon for a bow.

Method

1 Remove any leaves low down on your stems and any vicious thorns if you are using roses. Have your twine close to hand.

2 Place the cellophane flat on a table. Fold over end-to-end and mark the centre with a crease, then unfold.

3 Lay your strong stem of foliage centrally on the cellophane, at least 5 cm down from the crease.

4 Take your five flowers with strong stems and create an outline within which your other plant material can be placed. Lay the first stem to the right, barely shorter than the foliage. The second should be placed to the left. Work outwards and downwards with the remaining stems to establish an open 'V'. Graduate the heights gently, ensuring that all the stems cross at approximately the same point low down.

5 Place at least half of your round flowers in the wide spaces between the placements already made, again at varying heights and crossing as before.

6 Add two or three stems of your optional shorter foliage in a similar way and add the remainder of the round flowers. Do not allow your flowers to come down too low. Try to get your stems crossing at approximately the same place. Add more foliage if appropriate.

7 Place your more delicate flowers on top, angling them so that each one is shown to its best advantage.

8 Tie the stems in place with raffia, twine or string or an electrician's tie.

9 Fold the top half of the cellophane back over the flowers. Staple the sides down in four or five places but not so completely that the air cannot enter.

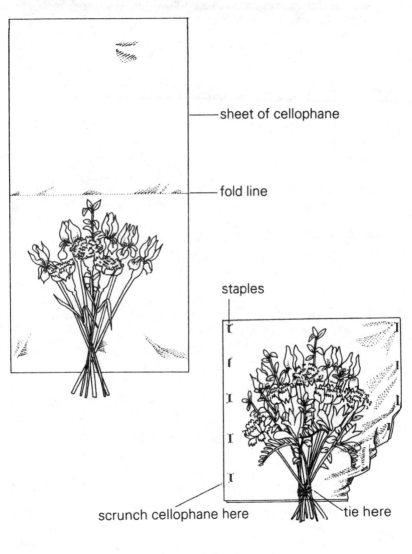

sheet of cellophane

fold line

staples

scrunch cellophane here tie here

A presentation wrap

10 Scrunch up the cellophane at the point where you have tied the stems and tie. You need to have plenty of space within your 'bag' so that the flowers can breathe. Trim the stem ends and cellophane and add your ribbon bow.

How to make a simple bow

1 For a bow of approximately 10 cm in diameter you will need about two metres of inexpensive polypropylene ribbon, available from florists, specialist ribbon shops or flower club sales tables. Polypropylene ribbon is widely used by florists. It is inexpensive and can be torn into narrow strips quite easily, without damaging the edges.

2 Measure 10 cm from the free end of the ribbon and roll your long end round and round this length, thus keeping the flattened roll 10 cm long.

3 When all the ribbon has been used, create a gentle crease across the centre by folding one end of the roll over to meet the other.

4 Take a sharp pair of scissors and cut two shallow 'V's inwards but stopping short of the centre.

centre crease   cut along dotted line

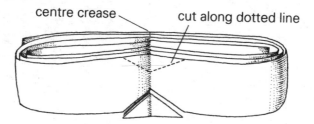

5 Take a new, thinner piece of the ribbon, wrap it tightly round the centre of your bow and tie, leaving two long loose ends.

6 Place your fingers inside the bow and pull the innermost loop out, at the same time giving it a twist of 45°.

Flowers in a vase: a monochromatic colour scheme with cow parsley in abundance

Flowers in a vase: bear grass adds flowing movement

The elongated triangle arrangement

This *pot-et-fleur* demonstrates the impact of five gerberas amongst
houseplants

A basket of flowers picked from the countryside

A circular table arrangement reflects a spring garden scene

For this pedestal arrangement, large-headed roses and hydrangea are in scale with stately delphiniums

Miniature roses emphasise the delicacy of this cup and saucer design

Left: a fragrant topiary tree with rosemary and lavender. Right: a cone of ivy leaves with poppy seed-heads

A fruit and vegetable design creates a spectacular display

This Christmas ring combines dried and fresh material

A festive garland of blue spruce is ready to festoon a doorway or fireplace

7   Repeat until all the loops have been drawn out, alternating the
    sides. Gently tease and twist your loops to form a uniform bow.
8   The two long loose ends can be used to tie round a gift such as
    the presentation wrap or tied bunch above.

17

—— SPRING ——
FLOWERS

Daffodils and other bulb flowers do more than anything to announce the start of a new growing season, even though current production techniques mean that they are on sale earlier and for longer. Spring brings hope and renewal. Nothing brightens a cold room better than a bunch of daffodils, perhaps simply arranged in a glass container. Adding several stems to a *pot-et-fleur* gives instant sunshine. Here are some other quick ideas to show off your flowers and skills.

- If you live in a flat, take a small terracotta pot with you when visiting a friend in the country in early spring. Line the bottom of the pot with broken crocks or small pieces of polystyrene. Fill the pot three quarters full with soil. Dig up a small turf with daisies growing amongst the grass and push this down onto the soil. With watering this will last until many more flowers are available.

- For Easter buy a branch of contorted willow which has twisted branches. This is available from many florists. Place the branch securely in a terracotta pot containing foam which is flush with or slightly lower than the rim. Cover the foam with moss. Suspend eggs on ribbons or tie yellow bows or yellow feathers at intervals on the branches.

- A mass of cow parsley or tall field buttercups can be placed in a jam jar. This can then be placed inside a tall basket, terracotta pot or copper container. If you need to disguise the top of the jam jar stick some Sellotape across it at intervals and rest some moss on top.

- Create a crescent with two pieces of curved pussy willow on a pinholder. Take five, or perhaps seven, daffodils or tulips and place them at different heights through the centre, between the outline material. Add three large leaves at the base.

A spring crescent arrangement

Spiral of daffodils

Daffodils have soft hollow stems so they are difficult to arrange in foam. Arranging them in a spiral on a pinholder shows off all the different angles of the daffodil and provides exciting interest.

Components

The components are as follows:

- About fifteen daffodils, out of the bud stage. At least four should have long stems.
- A pinholder.
- A flat dish.
- Several large pebbles or flatish stones.

Method

1   Secure your pinholder well to the base of a flat dish.
2   Lay the stems out on a table and cut each one so that each stem is slightly longer than the next.
3   Place the longest stem centrally on the pinholder.
4   Rotate your container and pinholder forty-five degrees and insert the second stem.
5   Turn the container another forty-five degrees and insert the third stem.
6   Continue turning and adding your daffodils, building up the spiral.
7   Complete the design by placing flat stones at the bottom to give good balance and to hide your mechanics.

A spiral of daffodils

Easter nest

This is an extremely simple yet very effective and different design. It can be kept from year to year and still look spring-like. It can be placed on a windowsill, sideboard or on top of a television set.

Components

The components are as follows:

- Silver birch branches, two or three about a metre long. Silver birch is ideal as it is strong yet flexible. Willow breaks too easily.
- A nest, purchased or made from hay and perhaps some furry chicks or some small Easter eggs.
- A length of ribbon (optional).

Method

1 Gently bend the branches of birch so that the ends meet and cross.
2 Tie the stems together where they cross. Ensure there is enough fullness so that your branches 'sit' upright comfortably. If they

An Easter nest

seem loathe to sit firm, persist by teasing them apart to create a flat base. You may have to stick a piece of fix to the underside.

3   Rest your nest and/or eggs in the centre.
4   If you wish, tie a ribbon round the point where your stems cross.

—— Circular table arrangement ——

A spring garden scene for a table is particularly lovely to look down upon and is always popular. It is easily put together with bits and pieces from the garden and can be with or without candles. Whoever visits will comment on this design.

Components

- A round plastic casement ring containing foam which rises about 2.5 cm above the rim. They are available with different diameters. The 25 cm or 30 cm are useful sizes. Such rings are not always easy to find but search around for they are for sale and worth finding. Try florists or large garden centres. They can be used more than once. When it is too full of holes to use again take out the old foam and put in new, carved from a block of foam to fit the circle.
- Some candles (optional) – lemon or yellow candles add to the spring-time mood.
- A variety of spring flowers, such as flowering currant, muscari, kerria, forsythia, winter jasmine, hellebores or miniature daffodils.
- Some foliage – roundish leaves such as ivy and short sprigs of filler foliage such as euonymus, evergreen hebe or pittosporum.
- Bark, dried fungi, dried seed heads, fruit, larch cones and/or walnuts to add interest through a change of texture or form, and which will make your flowers and foliage go further.

Method

There are many different ways of creating your design. One way is to use candles and to keep your material low and approximately the same height. Another is to vary the height of your plant material considerably.

A circular table arrangement with candles

The use of taller material would make the addition of candles impractical and dangerous. Methods using (a) candles and (b) plant material of different heights work well.

(a) With candles

1 Wet your ring but do not oversoak.
2 Put your candles in position. Use the specially-designed candle holders or cocktail sticks on tape. Slender candles look good in this design and can be inserted straight into the foam. They look effective in twos or threes. Be careful using four placements of candles except in an Advent ring (see page 141). Four placements create a square and a square on a round prevents the eye travelling round the design as smoothly. Three, five or six placements work well.
3 Insert one clump of flowers on short stems. Cover the rim both on the inside and outside of the ring.
4 Work round the ring adding your groupings of plant material. Think carefully about your use of colour, texture and contrast of forms. Make good use of plain round overlapping leaves, pieces of fungi or small pieces of bark to create the quiet areas and to give

interesting contrast to the freshness and form of your spring flowers.

5 Lift the circle occasionally to see it at eye level. Ensure that the material covers the rim of the foam container.

(b) With plant material of different height

The method is the same, but here the stems of the plant material come into play. Allow plant material with longer stems to give height instead of the candles.

18
—— SUMMER ——
FLOWERS

Summer is the time when garden flowers are at their most abundant and there is an array of inexpensive material in the flower shops. The leaves of deciduous trees are sufficiently mature to last well when cut and arrangements can be big and beautiful. The rock gardens and the flower borders are full of delights for exquisite small arrangements. Try the following ideas:

- For a table centrepiece place a thick church candle on a plate. Encircle it with foliage and roses. If possible, tuck the rose stem ends under the leaves into orchid or cigar tubes, a little hidden foam or a small amount of water.

- Large shells from the beach can be grouped together on a flat dish or base. Trails of honeysuckle can be arranged over the shells with their stem ends in orchid tubes hidden between the shells.
- Sweet peas can be massed in a glass vase with clear marbles as the mechanics. The light in a bright room will reflect all the wonderful colours of your sweet peas through the marbles and you will be enhancing the delicate beauty of your flowers. By picking sweet peas from the garden you are encouraging more to grow.
- Make a ring of herbs. Take a metal coathanger and bend it into a circle. Bind small bunches of long lasting herbs such as rosemary, sage, marjoram, thyme and curry plant onto the ring with reel wire. Pack tightly and thickly as the herbs will shrink as they dry but the fragrance will remain.
- Use daisy chains as napkin rings or at the base of a candle.
- A few focal flower heads can be simply floated in a bowl with or without roundish leaves. Try roses, cornflowers or geums.

—————— Pedestal arrangement ——————

A pedestal is a column or pillar with an integral bowl, or a flat top to take a bowl, which will contain your arrangement. A pedestal design is tall, usually about two metres high. It therefore needs a lot of plant material, so summer is an ideal time to have a first attempt.

The pedestal

The most commonly seen pedestal is made of wrought iron. Most places of worship, whatever the denomination, have a pedestal lurking somewhere in the background. Wooden pedestals are often for sale in pine shops. Victorian or Regency pedestals are sometimes for sale in antique shops. At the other end of the market is a DIY version consisting of an empty carpet tube fixed onto a plinth with a flat board attached to the top. A raised bird table is ideal for practice and even for the real event. If there is no integral bowl you will need a flat-bottomed bowl for your design. A good sized bowl is about 20 cm wide and 9 cm deep. Many plastic bulb bowls are about this size.

If you use a bowl approximately 20 cm wide and 9 cm deep you will need one and three quarter blocks of foam. The full block is placed upright on a frog, at the back of the bowl. The other block – only about three quarters will fit – should be placed lengthways on its side onto another frog in front of it.

You will then need an amount of 25 mm mesh wire netting. Many ironmongers do not like to sell this in amounts of less than a metre. Cut off the amount needed to cover your foam as a 'cap'. You will need to cut off the thick selvedge. The netting can be kept securely in place by means of reel wire, which can be purchased from a flower club sales table, or thin string or rubber bands. The wire or string should be wound round a strand of netting on one side, then passed under the bowl, round the stem of the pedestal and then round to the wire netting on the other side. Repeat on the other two sides for extra security. If you are using rubber bands, interloop them under the bowl and bring them up over the foam and netting to keep the netting in place.

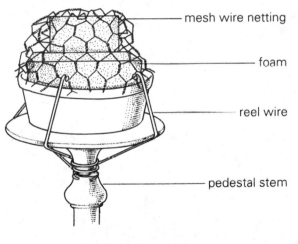

mesh wire netting

foam

reel wire

pedestal stem

Pedestal mechanics

Shape and scale

The vast majority of pedestal arrangements have a symmetrical shape. They are an enlargement of the symmetrical triangle arrangement or the circular arrangement. There must, however, be a strong emphasis on trailing plant material flowing down from the foam to create a 'skirt'. Summer trails could be periwinkle, fragrant honeysuckle or blackberry blossom and are used in addition to the outline stems.

Every piece of plant material you use should be in scale. Any stem which has neat foliage in a slim line will not work as well as one with a fuller shape which would be too heavy for a small table arrangement. Camellia, eleagnus and ivy sprays will work better than ceanothus, cotoneaster, berberis or winter jasmine which have small neat leaves and flowers.

For the outline in summer take advantage of the branches from trees such as dogwood (cornus), weigela, green beech and lime. Stripped of its rather sticky leaves the lime gives an exciting look to an arrangement. Whitebeam, which is now being planted more and more in urban areas because of its tolerance to pollution, comes into leaf early and its leaves last well even in early summer. Prune carefully, ensuring that you do not take more than the tree can stand or so much that its shape is spoilt.

Stiff line foliage such as yucca and iris leaves are difficult to incorporate into a graceful pedestal design. They are too uncompromisingly rigid. For the same reason gladioli, as line flowers, can be difficult to use.

Method

Your placements are the same as for the symmetrical triangle (chapter 5), only on a larger scale. The only difference is that stems (b) and (d) need to be extended to flow down the pedestal stand as in the diagram opposite. Once stem placements (a), (b), (c) and (d) are in place they need to be reinforced. This can be done by:

- Placing stem (e) behind stem (a), angled slightly backwards to give depth. It should be shorter than stem (a).
- Angling stems (f) backwards to give depth and to give substance to your triangle.
- Filling out your 'skirt' by placing stems (g) at the back, the sides and the front of the design to give downward flow and thus an unregimented, graceful appearance. Very approximately you will need about thirteen stems. The length of your stems is unimportant but big pedestal arrangements are beautiful.

Line flowers to reinforce the shape made by the foliage could be delphiniums, larkspur or perhaps eremurus. Foxgloves are superb. Lupins look lovely initially but are rather wayward. As with tulips, when you come to admire or worry about your arrangement the next day, you might well find that your carefully arranged shape has totally altered.

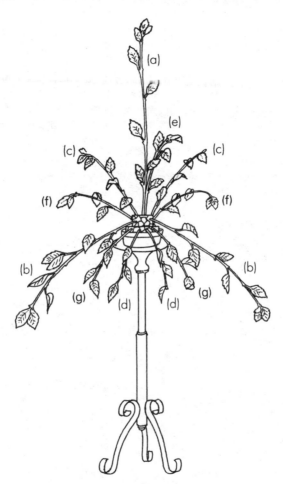

You will need approximately ten or fifteen large concealer leaves. Bergenia, fatsia or one of the larger hostas would be more suitable than geranium leaves, tolmeia or those of the flowering currant. These are so important. They cover the foam and netting, give depth at the back and frame the beauty of your flowers and other foliage. Please do use them.

Focal flowers could be peonies, hydrangeas – although these last better when cut in late summer – or zinnias. Roses are particularly lovely in pedestals at this time of year. If your blooms are not large enough, then group several together for greater impact.

Cow parsley in early summer and stems of *Alchemilla mollis* in mid-to late summer are the most perfect filler materials that you could ever wish for. Cow parsley with its creamy heads and *Alchemilla* with its lime-green flowers give an airiness and joy to any arrangement and in pedestals a thrilling extra dimension. *Alchemilla mollis* can now be bought from some florists during the summer months. Try to get longer rather than shorter stems and if the stems are a bit sparse use two or three stems together.

Other filler material could be clarkia or stocks – whatever is cheap and plentiful. Spotted laurel, wild or cultivated rhododendron or perhaps mahonia could be added to give bulk, particularly at the back of your design. Amaranthus with its drooping tassels looks lovely and in late summer lasts extremely well.

Your pedestal is going to be viewed at a distance so keep walking away to look at it from where you think the majority of people will see it. It is amazing how different it can look.

Do ensure that the sides and back of your pedestal are full. Do not fill the back upwards with too many flat pieces of conifer. Use colour and downward flowing material to create depth and, through depth, greater interest.

When your arrangement is complete, fill the bowl with water. All the stems will take up a lot of water so every day ensure that there is some water in the bottom of the bowl.

────── Sweet-smelling topiary tree ──────

Topiary trees come in all shapes and sizes. The most usual shape in flower arranging is a round 'ball' impaled on a branch or stem which represents the tree trunk. A 1.5 metre topiary tree can grace a wedding marquee or stately home whilst its 15 cm brother can add interest to a bedsit. The principles are the same.

Components

For a tree about 30 cm high your mechanics will be:

- A container to take your tree. It is best to use a cheap plastic pot with an opening of about 9 cm in diameter which can then be placed inside an attractive outer container.
- Plaster of paris or Polyfilla.
- A thick branch, with or without a gentle curve, at least 2.5 cm in diameter and about 22 cm long. As an alternative you could use several twigs or stems of bamboo bunched together to give one thick stem. It is easier to impale the foam onto the branch if it is sawn to a rough point at one end. If you or a friend are good at DIY hammer a long nail through the branch about 2–3 cm from the end or make a hole with a drill. This nail is to prevent the foam sliding down the branch. It can be difficult to get a nail through a branch so do not worry if you cannot.
- A cylinder of foam, well soaked.
- A piece of thin plastic bag such as that used by dry cleaners to protect clothes.
- About thirty to seventy short stems of rosemary or other fragrant herbs. Rosemary is ideal for topiary trees as it has a strong stem, is fragrant and will dry in situ, giving a framework for the later addition of dried flowers. The bushier your material the fewer stems you will need. Young growth will quickly wilt but can easily be trimmed from the longer-lasting mature growth. Fresh lavender flower stems would also be lovely but you will need many more stems.
- Approximately twelve small to medium fresh focal flowers, and/or about twenty short pieces of escallonia or other strong-stemmed flowers. Alternatively use dried flowers such as roses (optional).

Method

1   Place some stones, or alternatively small pieces of broken poly-styrene plant holder, into the bottom of your pot. Mix plaster of paris or Polyfilla with water to a stiff paste. Place about 3 cm in the bottom, and insert the blunt end of your branch. Add sufficient plaster of paris or Polyfilla so that your container is three quarters full. Hold the branch in place for several minutes until happily upright. Leave until the branch is firmly set in your mix. Depending on how wet your mixture is this will take about one hour.

2   Wrap the thin plastic carefully round the foam and keep it in place with a small amount of tape. This will slow down water evaporation from the foam. Use as little tape and plastic as possible as any extra thickness makes it more difficult to insert the stems. Impale the foam carefully on the pointed end and rest it on the nail.

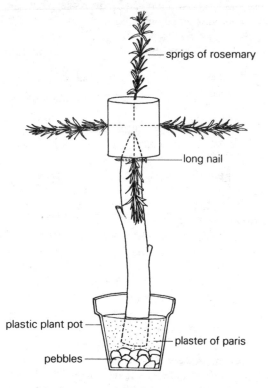

A topiary tree – the first four stems in place

3 Insert your first stems in the four directions, north, south, east and west. This will loosely determine the overall size of your finished 'ball'. Gradually fill in your ball. Do not work too conscientiously at one area or your ball will not be uniform. When you have a full shape trim with scissors to give a rounder shape. Pack your ball tightly as all plant material shrinks when it dries.

4 If you wish you can add interest with roses and/or other fresh flowers, such as short stems of flowering escallonia.

5 If you wish your rosemary to dry in situ you will need to add some dried flowers to hide the gaps which will appear when the rosemary dries and also to heighten the interest.

6 Place the pot into a more attractive outer container. If this container is too large, place some foam or a saucer inside to raise the tree to the required level. Cover the foam with bun or reindeer moss, pebbles or shells, to hide the plaster of paris.

Whatever the season, a topiary tree can be created from evergreen material. Short bushy line material which is long-lasting or which will dry in the foam and remain attractive is perhaps the easiest to use. Examples are yew, box, osmanthus, myrtle and conifer.

If you have a standard bay tree in a pot, try pushing stems of white carnations or white daisy chrysanthemums into the shrubbery for an instant summery effect for a grand occasion. These flowers will last without water for a few hours if they are not placed in full sunlight.

———— Cup and saucer design ————

This design is a microcosm of summer. Whereas the pedestal arrangement shows the abundance of summer, this design makes use of the smaller treasures you will find in your garden and windowboxes at this time of year.

Components

Your mechanics are simple. You will need:

- A cup and saucer, any size or colour.
- Half a frog or a drawing pin.
- A tiny amount of foam.

- Some flowers or foliage which will be in scale with your cup and saucer. The colour of your china or pottery should be repeated in the plant material you use.

The flowers from rock gardens are especially suitable as many have wiry stems which are easily inserted in foam and are long-lasting. Examples are bugle, the delicate flowers of aquilegia (Granny's bonnet), pinks, fuchsia, cranesbill, gypsophila, heuchera (coral flower), feverfew, London pride, herbs, miniature roses, jasmine and forget-me-nots. The list is never-ending. These are just ideas. You should use what you have or search the hedgerows for the treasures which lie there.

Method

The first decision is how you wish to arrange the cup and saucer. You could have:

- The flowers spilling out of the bowl of the cup.
- The cup turned upside down, for most cups have a natural mini reservoir for water. Simply place your cup upside down on the saucer and create a downward cascade as in (*a*) below. If your cup is small use a drawing pin to hold your piece of foam instead of a frog.

(a)

The handles of a few cups are fixed at an angle which prevents the cup lying flat. If so you can try another way:

- The cup placed sideways on the saucer resting at a slight upward angle, on the two cut-off prongs of a frog as in (*b*) below. Place a small piece of foam on the full length prongs and arrange your plant material in an upward crescent, following the circle of your opening. A little piece of fix can be placed under the base of the cup to hold it in place.

(b)

This design can be arranged in any season. In spring with heather, lily of the valley, grape hyacinths or snowdrops. In autumn with gleanings from the garden and in winter perhaps with dried flowers. Summer however provides the range and colour to complement any cup and saucer. Do try it.

19

AUTUMN FLOWERS

Autumn flowers and foliage with their glowing colours are spectacular. Early autumn is a time of abundance. The harvested fruit and vegetables are in perfect harmony with plant material. Harvest and Thanksgiving ceremonies take place all over the world. Pedestals overflowing with berries and sprays of fruit such as crab apples or old man's beard give focus to any display. Here are some other ideas:

- Gourds are so simple to grow. When harvested in the autumn they can be placed in a large fruit bowl with perhaps a few leaves of varying hues. The only problem with gourds is that they need a large area in which to grow – allotments are perfect.
- Pumpkins, marrows, even peppers and grapefruit can be hollowed out to form containers for your flowers. They look effective but are short-lived as mould will quickly form on their interiors. So scoop out as much flesh as you can. Place a jam jar or container filled with water inside and add nasturtiums, geraniums or marigolds with their warm and vibrant colours.
- For Remembrance Sunday the short-lived poppies are impossible to use in long-lasting arrangements. But large, fabric or paper poppies are a useful, long-term investment. When mixed in a large pedestal arrangement with glossy foliage, no one will be any the wiser. If they get crushed in the box, gentle steaming with a kettle will get them back into shape.
- Wisps of the rosebay willow herb with one or two red gerberas and a piece of charcoaled wood can add atmosphere to a Bonfire Night party.

───── Fruit and vegetable raised ─────
display

This is a large exciting display which is economical and long-lasting. Your container is composed of a matching dinner plate, side plate and saucer and two empty toilet rolls. Cover the toilet rolls in a fabric to tone with your room, plates or the fruit and vegetables which you will be using. The fabric will also give your toilet rolls extra strength. Place the first one on the upturned dinner plate. Balance the side plate on the roll. Add the second roll and finally the saucer. No other mechanics should be needed but if you feel uncertain, give extra stability with some fix. The example in the colour section is balanced without fix

You then need to add your fruit and vegetables. Choosing fruit and vegetables for an arrangement can be just as exciting as choosing flowers. There are so many fruits and vegetables available now in the most glorious colours, shapes and textures. Large supermarkets, well-stocked greengrocers and market stalls are the places to scour. Avoid using fruit and vegetables all of a similar shape. The rounded shapes of apples, oranges and tangerines appear more interesting if bananas and grapes are added for contrast. Remember that the eye spends longer looking at a rough texture than a smooth one. Think also about passion fruit, courgettes, squash, star fruit and broccoli.

Start with your dinner plate. Use a frog, secured with fix, on which you can impale a piece of fruit or a vegetable. Perhaps start with the strong form of an orange. It is important to get the first piece firmly

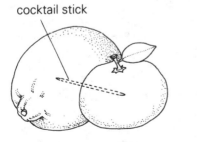

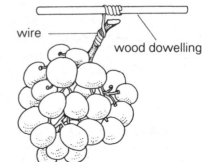

Linking and securing pieces of fruit

in position so that the other pieces can be built up, one resting against the other. If necessary use cocktail sticks or thin dowelling to link one fruit with another. Try not to think of the problems this could lead to if an unknowing guest helps himself uninvited to your centrepiece! Wood does not damage the fruit so it can be eaten later. However if metal skewers are inserted the fruit will become inedible.

Grapes might need some support. So wire a cocktail stick onto the main stem and then impale another fruit with the long end.

When all three dishes are filled to your satisfaction, with a good mix of form, texture and colour, tuck in some leaves. Any autumnal leaves will enhance your design. The leaves of Virginia creeper last well into autumn and are a particularly lovely shape to complement that of your container. A few leaves from the roadside or hedgerow will also give a good foil. Try sprays of blackberries, green tomatoes or hops. Sprays of pyracantha, rowan or skimmia berries or perhaps rosehips can be tucked between the fruits. If you prefer, put the ends into an orchid tube or cigar holder. A few late nasturtiums or geraniums can be included in the same way. Avoid flowers which are susceptible to the ethylene gas given off by all fruit and vegetables (see page 20). Chrysanthemums and roses are reasonably tolerant.

———————— Cone arrangement ————————

This is an exciting design for displaying autumn foliage and some choice seasonal flowers or fruit. It is ideal for a buffet party when space is limited and you would like to have something a little different. As it can be viewed from any direction it can be placed centrally on a table.

If a small cone is required, of no more than 25 cm, then a block of foam can be sculpted into the required shape. The cone should have a fairly slim tall shape, as a squat one will lose its conical appearance once plant material has been added.

For a larger cone you will need wire netting to give extra support, moulded so that it forms a cone shape.

All the small, seemingly useless pieces of foam that you have been accumulating over the previous chapters in this book can now be put to good use! They must be well soaked and pushed, even squashed, into your wire netting cone so that it becomes a solid mass with no gaps.

The cone can be placed on a low plastic dish. But for maximum impact raise it on a terracotta pot. To keep it securely in place fill the pot with dry foam used for dried flower arrangements. Then insert the loose netting ends from the base of the cone into the foam. The top of the pot can later be covered with moss.

It is now time to cover the cone. Various plant materials can be used. Very small snips of conifer are excellent for covering, as are neat round ivy leaves. For a different effect use variegated leaves. Try to use only one type of foliage. It is much easier and very effective. Start at the bottom and with your first circle overlap the bottom ridge of wire netting. The stems need to be sharply angled upwards to keep a neat conical shape. Work upwards. It is simple until the last couple of placements at the summit which need a little bit of manipulation, so save some good shaped pieces.

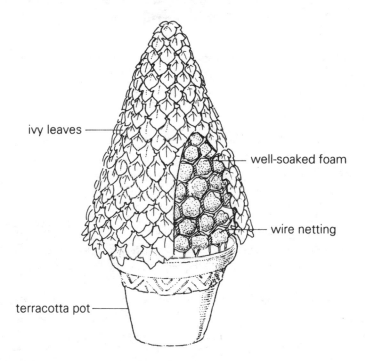

ivy leaves

well-soaked foam

wire netting

terracotta pot

Once your base is in place, especially if you have used bright foliage, you might decide that you wish for nothing more. However, here are two delightful ways of finishing an autumn cone:

- Add flat short heads of autumn focal flowers, such as small single dahlias or the round flowers of spray chrysanthemums.
- Get some cocktail sticks and insert fruit such as crab apples or kumquats. For a larger cone try small tangerines. Spear them with a cocktail stick, cut the end to an appropriate length and insert them at regular intervals into the cone.

Your cone, without flowers, can last for months in a cool conservatory or outdoors. You could ring the changes with fruits, berries and flowers. The basic cone arrangement can be doused under water from time to time, or it can be sprayed.

—— Hydrangea arrangement with —— seedheads

Autumn is the time to pick hydrangeas. If picked when mature they can be the basis for an arrangement which will dry in situ. You can pack them away after Christmas until the following year or alternatively use them to fill a fireplace or basket where they can stay for many months more.

Many consider that hydrangeas dry better cut on the old wood (wood that was formed in the previous year's growing season.) Hydrangeas are ideal when grown in tubs because you can create different colours by using different types of soil. An acid or peaty soil will produce bluer flowers and a more alkaline or chalky soil pinker flowers. Mass your flowers in any vase or container. If you are lucky enough to have a copper or brass kettle, jam pot or spill holder, the combination is stunning. Place your stems in wet foam or in 5 cm of water. There will be no need to add any further water. Remember that one and a half to two times the volume of flowers and foliage to the volume of the container will give good proportions.

Hydrangeas on their own form a stunning display. However, if you only have a few blooms add seedheads from the autumn hedgerow or river banks, possibly tall spikes of rusty sorrel, sprays of hips, haws or rowan and trails of wild clematis. The more mature the clematis, the more likely the seeds are to disperse when picked. Try spraying them with hair lacquer. Take a walk in the garden or countryside and add what you find to your arrangement.

20
—— WINTER AND ——
CHRISTMAS FLOWERS

In winter and for the festive season, new dimensions open up to flower arrangers. They are able to combine their knowledge of arranging with design and craftwork to create a joyful house during the cold winter months. Winter is the time when flowers become more expensive, but so much can be created from nature's free gifts – pine cones, nuts and berries – which, together with baubles, ribbons and a little spray paint can be used for some quick and simple ideas.

The following will be useful additions to your winter arrangements.

—————————— Pine cones ——————

Pine cones give wonderful textural interest to any design and a feeling of warmth and comfort. All cones are useful whatever their shape or size but do leave some for the insects and animals who use them as food. Pine cones can be left their natural colour or sprayed gold or silver. Put the cones in a box to spray them as this will localise the spread of the paint and therefore cause less mess and save more paint. Alternatively, dab the tips of the scales with gym shoe whitener to give a subtle effect of snow.

To give an artificial stem to cones they need to be wired. Below are two methods. The more open a cone is the easier it is to wire. Wires can be purchased in varying thicknesses or gauges. The two most useful gauges for cones and ribbons are perhaps the 0.71 mm and the

0.90 mm. The 0.71 mm is suitable for smaller cones and ribbon loops. The 0.90 mm is thicker and is useful for larger, heavier cones. If in doubt ask your florist or the lady behind the sales table at your local flower club.

- For small to medium-sized cones wrap a wire round the lowest part of the cone, between the scales, pulling it tight but leaving each end loose. Take the loose ends, bring them both together under the base of the cone and twist to form your stalk.

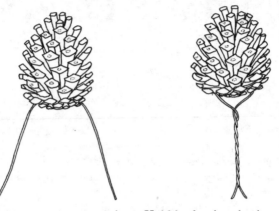

- For larger cones use two wires. Hold both wires horizontally, one each side of the cone and force each one as low as possible between the scales. Twist the two ends at each side together. Pull under the base of the cone and twist together to form a stalk.

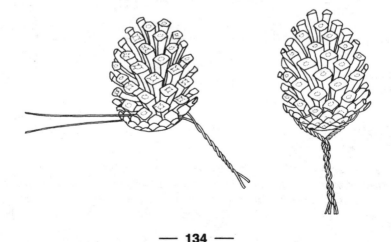

———————————— Nuts ————————————

Beech nuts usually have a short stalk which is just sufficient to poke into foam. If you need longer stalks, take a wire and pass it over and down between the 'petals' and form a stalk by twisting one side of the wire round the other.

Walnuts are easy. Insert a strong wire or cocktail stick through the join on the base of the walnut and add a dab of glue to keep it securely in place. Brazil nuts and almonds are tough and need a drill to make a hole before a wire can be inserted.

———————————— Berries ————————————

Privet berries

Privet berries often go unnoticed but the shiny black berries are most attractive. Remove some or all of the leaves.

Ivy seedheads

Ivy seedheads are produced in abundance once this climber rises above its support, such as a fence or a tree. They look lovely sprayed gold or silver.

Fatsia and fatshedera seedheads

Fatsia and fatshedera seedheads are similar to the ivy seedheads but larger.

Holly berries

Holly berries are wonderful but birds do need them and will probably take them anyway! Artificial red berries bought in clusters from a flower club sales table or specialist shop would deceive all but the canniest of birds.

Foliage

Variegated foliage

Variegated foliage is always useful to the flower arranger and no more so than in winter when it brightens the garden and adds impact to flower arrangements when flowers are expensive. Three superb variegated foliages are:

- *Euonymus japonicus* 'Aureo-picta'
- *Elaeagnus pungens* 'Maculata'
- *Hedera helix* 'Goldheart'

Holly and ivy

Both can be found in the majority of our hedgerows. Variegated holly grows very slowly but is a lovely shrub to have in the flower arranger's garden.

Conifer

This is the time of year when conifer really comes into its own. It has a winter 'feel', so much so that at other times of the year it can look as if it is only used because no other foliage is available. It can last for months. There are many different forms of conifer, many of which have exciting colours: rich greens, golds, blue-greens as well as the plain greens. The latter can always be purchased from florists. Take care when cutting from a conifer, for if a large hole is made in the shrub it will never recover.

Ribbons

Ribbons not only make flowers go further but they can also turn an idea into a celebration. An easy example of how to make a bow from inexpensive ribbon is given in chapter 16. Ribbon loops are even simpler to make and are ideal to add to many of the ideas below. Use polypropylene ribbon as it can be easily torn to the required width, leaving smooth edges. Make one, two or more loops of the required size. One of the loose ends can be brought upwards to be included with the loops. Wrap a length of florists' wire firmly round the bottom and insert the wire ends, one twisted round the other, into your foam.

A ribbon loop

Paper ribbon is sold in rolls and is simple and effective to use. When it is unfurled a simple knot produces a stiff bow which can be added to basket handles, presentation wraps, topiary tree trunks and even used as curtain tie backs.

—— Baubles and artificial material ——

Baubles provide a festive splash of colour when added to Christmas arrangements. Plastic ones are of course easier to use than metal ones. To include them in your arrangements you may need to add false stems. Place a length of florists' wire through the loop of the bauble and twist. To disguise the wire cover it with 'stem binding tape' which is widely used by florists. It is on a reel and can seem impossible to use correctly but keep on trying and the knack will come. Although stem tape comes in a variety of colours it is usually green. It is stretchy and if you pull it tightly and use warm hands it will cling round the wire as you turn it.

—— Quick and simple winter and —— Christmas ideas

Christmas tree

This is a hanging for your front door as an alternative to a wreath.

Make a double triangle of 1 cm wire netting with all sides approximately equal. Insert a 'trunk' of tree branch between the two thicknesses of netting and secure it in place with wire or perhaps freezer bag ties. Use short pieces of conifer to fill in your tree. To start insert the three placements as shown in the diagram and then work from the bottom upwards. Insert your stems at a sharp upward angle.

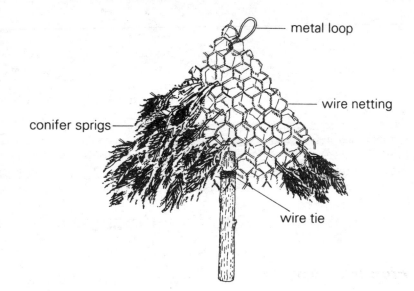

Fill it densely, weaving the pieces into your netting framework. Golden or rich green conifer is perfect for this tree and needs no further embellishment. You could however decorate your tree with small artificial berries, bows or mini baubles. By now your imagination will feel confident enough to take over. An extended paper clip or a piece of wire can be looped through the tip of your tree and then onto a nail in your door. With regular spraying your tree will last for months.

Horizontal decoration

A window-sill decoration

Take two pieces of long-lasting blue spruce which is available from many florists during the Christmas season. Place them end-to-end with one stem overlapping the other by a few inches. Bind them firmly together with wire or twine. Wire some cones, baubles, artificial fruits and/or ribbon loops and attach them to the spruce stems in the central area. This gives a lovely elongated design for a window-sill or as a table centrepiece.

Festive pot-et-fleur

Substitute a red poinsettia for one of the pot plants in your *pot-et-fleur* and add a large red or red and gold bow. Alternatively add a peach poinsettia with a peach bow. (Do not purchase a poinsettia which has been standing outside a shop. Poinsettias are very susceptible to draughts and are very likely to collapse as soon as you get them home.)

Fruit and baubles

Add a few baubles and sprigs of long lasting evergreens, such as laurel or camellia, to a basket or bowl of fruit.

Church candles in terracotta pots

Church candles are a rich cream colour and come in various thick-nesses. If you have a problem finding them, ask your local church for the name of their suppliers. They give a wonderful atmosphere, especially when the wax has started to create intricate patterns down the sides. Fill a terracotta pot level with foam. Deeply insert the candle and cover the foam with moss. Insert short lengths of wire bent into a hairpin shape into the foam to keep the moss in place. A large pot can contain a grand old candle or you can create mini arrangements and use each one as part of an individual place setting at a dinner table.

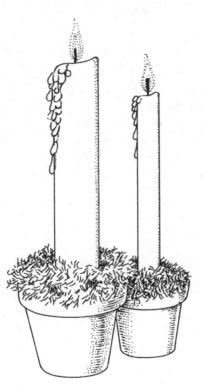

Candles, fruit and evergreens

Group candles of different shapes and sizes – perhaps in tints, tones and shades of one colour – on a board or tray. You can secure the candles to the board with some hot wax or fix. Add a few apples to a green design, lemons to a yellow one and tangerines to an orange one. Complete with tucks of conifer or laurel.

Festive circular arrangement

Make the circular arrangement described on page 114 but use thin red candles with perhaps holly and berries. Alternatively, place one large thick candle in the centre of the ring. Advent is the time to use four candles placed at regular intervals.

Table mat decoration

Make a ring of laurel or camellia leaves round a circular mat for each place setting. Sew the leaves together with strong green thread.

Baubles and branches in a glass vase

Place some plastic shiny baubles in a large glass vase. Place colourful cornus (dogwood) stems or some dried branches, sprayed silver or gold, in the vase using the baubles to help keep your stems in place.

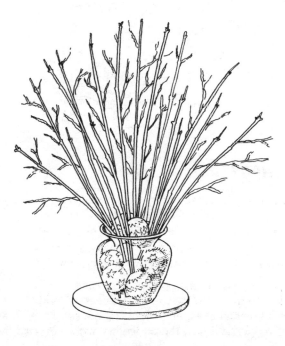

Individual trees in terracotta pots

Buy mini terracotta pots and fill them with dry or wet foam. Insert two or three sprigs of heather centrally in the foam. You could also use conifer. Decorate with mini bows or artificial holly berries. You could tie a ribbon round the tree 'trunks'.

Fresh garland

Garlands are an elongated flexible design which can be used to decorate a fireplace, a picture or a door frame. One of the easiest fresh garlands to make can be created from a thin rope or pairs of old tights knotted together. Attach your length to perhaps a door knob and a chair. Choose your length according to what you wish to decorate.

You will need several thick branches of conifer. They can be cut into several hundred small sprigs, a few centimetres long. The sprigs should be submerged under water for several hours. Take about five small sprigs of conifer and bind them together with thin wire. Make fifty to one hundred of these bundles. Begin building up your garland by binding a bundle onto the rope with reel wire. Start at the centre. Place the second bundle to face the first so that the two overlap. Work outwards from the centre, adding a few bunches to the left and then the same amount to the right so that the garland is symmetrical. Ensure that your tights or rope are well covered.

Alternatively, cut down the sides of a black plastic binliner so that it opens out into one long rectangular piece. Place a piece of blue spruce about 30 cm long over one end of the bag so that two-thirds of the tip protrudes. Scrunch up the bag behind the end of the stem. Use twine or reel wire to wrap the bag securely to the spruce. The bag should form a strong backing but is not seen from the front. Take two smaller pieces of spruce about 20 cm long and place them to overlap your first placement, one angled slightly to the right and one to the left. Pull your wire firmly over the stem ends to secure. Repeat until you reach the centre of the bag. Starting at the other end, repeat the process. At the centre carefully arrange your last piece over the worst of the stem ends.

Decorate your garlands with tangerines and apples on wooden skewers, ribbon, cones, or cinnamon sticks bound with raffia and wired.

Basket of pine cones

Fill a basket with pine cones which have been sprinkled with pine cone oil. Scented oils are available from gift shops and some chemists. Tuck in a few sprays of dried or fresh gypsophila and add shiny red apples or baubles.

Table centrepiece

For a round table centrepiece take a piece of foam and secure it well in a low container. Take about five short pieces of blue spruce and place out of the sides of the foam. Place one, two or three candles centrally and fill in with berries, variegated foliage, more spruce and perhaps some ribbon loops.

Oval door hanging

Plastic containers with handles are often used in churches to hang on the ends of pews. They can also be used at Christmas time for a quick and easy door hanging. Most flower club sales tables have these.

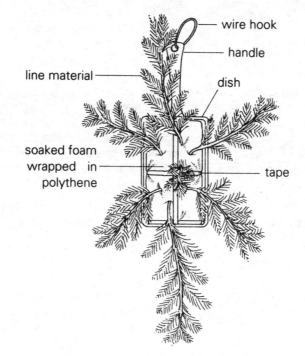

Twist a wire through the hole in the handle to form a hanging loop. This can be covered by stem binding tape. Wrap a piece of well soaked foam with thin polythene or cling film and secure firmly with florists' tape. Use as little tape as possible as this takes up 'stem space'. A third of a block will usually just fit this container yet rise well above it.

Create your horizontal arrangement as in chapter 3, but use wider spreading conifer or blue spruce as your line material. Add wired cones, perhaps sprayed gold, ribbon loops and variegated foliage. If so desired add curled ribbon trails. Fold a long piece of ribbon in half and cut the ends at an angle. Wire the folded end and insert out of the bottom of the foam, away from the handle. These trails can then be curled with a knife.

Flowers and baubles can be added. Hang it on the front door where it will last for weeks. Spray from time to time. As the handle is mostly concealed this design can also be placed horizontally as a table arrangement if the long ribbon trails are not added.

Christmas wreath

Take a coat hanger and push it out to form a circle. You will also need a bag of spagnum moss, which can be bought from many florists, and reel wire or a roll of garden twine.

Knot one end of your wire or twine to the frame where the handle joins. Take a large handful of damp moss, and squeeze it to form a hard mass. Place this on the wire circle and firmly wrap your wire or twine round and round, at about 2.5 cm intervals, pulling hard. Add more moss and repeat until your circle is complete. You now have a moss ring.

To neaten the back, bind on flat pieces of conifer using the same process.

Take some blue spruce and cut it into neat bushy pieces about 18 cm long. Still using the reel wire or twine, bind the spruce onto the ring on top of the moss. This is your basic wreath. It may be left as it is or decorated with cones, walnuts, small bows, artificial berries or perhaps tangerines impaled on cocktail sticks.

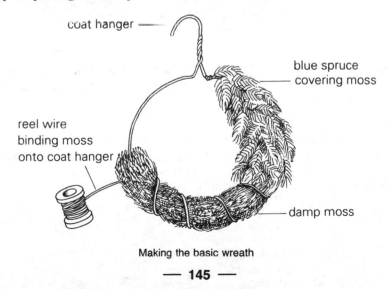

coat hanger —

blue spruce
— covering moss

reel wire
binding moss
onto coat hanger

— damp moss

Making the basic wreath

Night lights and evergreens

Group tumblers of coloured glass containing night lights on a bed of conifer or other long-lasting evergreens.

The Christmas tree – ideas for decoration

There are many theories on how to stop a fir dropping its needles. Try this one. Place the cut tree in a bucket of water. Wedge pieces of kindling wood in the bucket, around the base of the tree to keep it in place. The wood will swell with the water overnight and help to keep your trunk firmly in place. Despite the tree losing its roots the water seems to prevent the tree drying out as quickly.

Gypsophila
Take dried or fresh gypsophila and cut into pieces 18–26 cm long. Create a sweep of gypsophila with each piece 'hooked' onto the next. Entangled gypsophila is often a problem, but not in this instance.

Lavender
Bind small bunches of lavender or dried roses with ribbon and hang or place through your tree.

Ruscus
Ruscus can be purchased from many florists and lasts well out of water. Spray blue, silver or gold, whatever colour you desire and sweep it through your tree as you did with the gypsophila. It dries well and can be stored away for the following year.

Nuts
Spray nuts such as walnuts or pine cones to your desired colour or leave them natural. Glue a loop of narrow ribbon to the top of them and hang.

Pine cones
Spray your pine cones red. Drill a small hole in the base of your cone and insert a pipe cleaner. Add a dab of glue. Wrap the free end round your branch so that the cone stays firmly in place, either upright or hanging downwards. Glitter can be added the following year or the cones can be sprayed another colour.

—— APPENDIX 1 ——

—— Special conditioning ——

Berries

To minimise dropping, place a branch of berries in a solution of one part glycerine to two parts boiling water for twenty-four hours before arranging.

Carnations and spray carnations

Cut stems above the node. Cutting on the node or just below seems to restrict the uptake of water.

Gerberas

Gerberas are particularly sensitive to bacteria. Add one drop only of bleach to the water. To straighten, wrap in newspaper and place in deep water for twelve hours in a cool place. You can rest a food rack over the top of your bucket and thread the stems through into deep water.

Hellebores (Christmas and Lenten rose)

Early in the season they are extremely difficult to condition. Submerge for several hours under water. Ideally wait for the seed stage when they will last for weeks in water.

Hollow stems

All hollow-stemmed flowers such as lupins and delphiniums last longer if their stems are filled with water. Turn the stem upside down, insert a narrow funnel and fill with water. Plug with cotton wool.

Holly

Holly lasts longer out of water once it has been cut. Store it in a sheltered place covered with sacking.

Iris

If they show signs of not opening fully remove the calyx which surrounds the petals.

Lilies

The anthers bear pollen which stains not just clothes but wallpaper too. If you do have a stain do not try to wipe it off with a damp cloth but use a strip of Sellotape to lift it. Alternatively, hang the garment in the wind or sun and half a day later the stain should have gone.

Milky stems

The stems of some plants such as poppies, euphorbias and poinsettias contain a milky sap called *latex*. This sap contains particles of rubber. When the stem is cut the latex seals the stem and prevents the intake of water. There are two ways you can condition. Hold the stem in a flame from a gas stove or match until it sizzles. Repeat this process if you cut the stem again. Alternatively, place the stem end in hot water of about 60 degrees for a minute.

Mimosa

Mimosa needs to be in a moist atmosphere so buy it with the heads protected by a polythene bag and leave this on until you arrange your flowers.

Orchids

Orchids need a constant supply of water once cut which is why they are supplied with their own individual phials of water. When purchased, change the water but do not remove from the phial. Do not insert the stem end in foam if you can insert the phial still containing the stem in the foam.

Peony

To develop properly the buds need to be soft when purchased. Spray their heads with water.

Roses

To revive drooping roses cut the bottom 5 cm off the stems on the slant. Place the stem ends in a few centimetres of hot water at about 60 degrees, for about a minute. If the rose only has a short stem, protect the flower head with a paper bag. (A polythene bag would increase the humidity and encourage the development of botrytis. This is a prevalent grey mould which is encouraged to develop by high humidity and high temperature.) Alternatively, wrap the roses completely in newspaper and put in deep water in a cool place for at least twelve hours. If your roses have wilted once, they might again so you could hang them upside down to dry and use them in dried arrangements.

Spring flowers with heavy large foliage

Many spring flowers and flowering shrubs such as lilac, laburnum, philadelphus, *Viburnum opulus* and honesty have greedy leaves. Removing them means the water will all go to the flower heads and they will therefore last longer.

Tulips

If they droop and you want them straight, wrap them in damp newspaper up to the bottom of the flower head. Tie and leave in water in a cool place for about twelve hours. If they are ramrod straight and you want a curve, angle them in a vase so that the stem rests on the rim.

Wild flowers

Place in a plastic bag, ideally with a drop or two of water in it, and blow into it to cushion the flowers and to give them air. The air inside will become saturated with transpired water which will prevent evaporation. Too much water may mark the petals. Alternatively, for larger flowers wrap them in a cone of damp newspaper or wrap the stem ends in a damp tissue.

Wilted flowers

Recut the stem ends and place them in hot water of about 60 degrees for about a minute. You can also submerge the flower heads of hydrangeas and violets.

Young foliage

Place the cut stem ends in hot water of about 60 degrees for a minute then give them a drink in deep water in a cool place.

APPENDIX 2

Cultivated flowers and shrubs

The following are useful shrubs and flowers for flower arranging which can be grown in the garden or in tubs in many parts of the British Isles. The list is of course far from exhaustive. It includes a brief description of the shrub or flower and, where relevant, tips on how and where to grow it.

Line material

Berberis

Easy to grow evergreen and deciduous shrubs. Useful despite the spines which can make handling difficult.

Box

Slow-growing but very long-lasting when cut. Neat shiny leaves. Line in small arrangements, filler in larger arrangements. Sun or shade.

Broom

Curving line material with cream or yellow flowers spring/ early summer. Easy to grow. Sun.

Butcher's broom (ruscus)

The smooth variety *Ruscus hypoglossum* is easy to grow and long-lasting out of wa⁺ɘr. It will grow in dense shade.

Camellia

Needs an acid soil so in chalky areas should be grown in a container with lime free soil. Despite soil demands and the fact that it grows slowly, camellia must be included because of its glossy luxurious foliage which will keep for up to three months when cut if placed in a cool room, or left outside in a bucket until required. Plant it where it will not receive the early morning sun.

Ceanothus

Easy evergreen shrub with blue flowers spring or summer. Some varieties shade, most sun.

Cornus

A deciduous shrub which has leaves early in the year. Variegated and golden varieties. Stems sometimes red or black – they provide an interesting feature in the garden. Cuttings take easily. Can be cut back early spring to encourage new strong growth. Sun or shade.

Cotoneaster

Many varieties, evergreen and deciduous. Strong stems, with neat leaves, which last well when cut. Sunny position.

Elaeagnus

Variegated *Elaeagnus pungens* 'Maculata' has evergreen leaves heavily splashed with gold. It is a ray of sunshine during the drab winter months. Stiff stems excellent for pedestals and other large arrangements.

Escallonia

Neat arching evergreen branches. Pink, red or white flowers intermittently throughout the summer. Sunny site.

Forsythia

Bright yellow flowering shrub in early spring. Easy to grow.

Grevillea robusta

Silvery feathery evergreen.

Griselinia

Evergreen apple-green foliage. Good for coastal regions where it can be used as hedging. Needs some protection in colder areas until established. Sun or shade.

Kerria

Troublefree quick-growing deciduous shrub with bright yellow flowers in the early spring. Sun or shade.

Mahonia

Wide line for larger arrangements. An evergreen with leaflets coming off a main stem. Long-lasting with attractive yellow flowers in the winter. Will grow virtually anywhere and on any soil.

Quince (japonica, chaenomeles)

Strong stems of blossom in early spring. Lasts well in foam or water. Often the stems have a good curve. They produce edible fruits in the autumn.

Weigela

A deciduous shrub whose leaves develop early. Good-natured. Can easily be grown from cuttings. Mainly pink or white flowers which appear intermittently throughout the summer. Sun or partial shade.

Winter jasmine

Neat evergreen with pretty yellow flowers November to April. Grows anywhere.

Line flowers

Canterbury bells

Evergreen perennial. Pretty blue or white flowers on stiff tall stems which last well and keep flowering from June to August and beyond. Once in the garden they seed themselves and spread rapidly. Sun.

Chinese lanterns

Rapidly spreading plant which has inconspicuous flowers but wonderful orange calyxes surrounding the fruit in the autumn. These will dry in situ and retain their colour well. Shade.

Delphiniums

Perennial species may be raised from seed. Plants will produce flowers year after year in wonderful shades of white and blue. Sun.

Foxgloves

Easy to grow biennial which seeds itself once established. Spikes of long-lasting flowers. Seedheads useful for dried arrangements. Sun.

Lavender

Hardy evergreen shrub with fragrant flowers during the summer months. Delicate flower spikes mainly blue. If grown for drying, the deeper blue varieties are best. Butterflies and bees love lavender.

Solomon's seal

Arching sprays with bell-shaped flowers. Greenish-white in May. Lovely wherever but particularly in pedestals. Shade.

Concealer material

Arum

The *Arum italicum* 'Pictum' is a relation of the wild arum. It has narrow leaves, interestingly marbled throughout the winter months. The leaves die back in summer but spikes of red/orange berries appear. Grows in shade or deep shade.

Bergenia (elephants' ears)

Large low-growing evergreen leaves with red, pink or white flowers in early to late spring. Some varieties have reddish leaves during the winter months. Grows in sun or deep shade. Useful all the year round.

Conifer

All conifers are good for using in the winter, particularly around Christmas. Flower arrangers are usually better off with the quicker growers. Some grow terribly slowly. When planting make sure they are well watered in.

Epimedium (bishop's hat)

Evergreen wiry-stemmed leaves which have lovely autumn tints and shades. They spread easily and have pretty yellow, pink or red flowers. Partial shade.

Fatshedera

An extremely useful, easily grown shrub. A cross between an ivy and a fatsia and size-wise half way between the two. Long-lasting. Half shade or shade.

Fatsia

Large hand-shaped leaves ideal for large arrangements. Evergreen and pollution tolerant. Half shade or shade.

Heuchera

Very similar to tellima. Also easy-going. Coral red flowers on spikes during the summer months. The variety 'Palace Purple' has lovely dark red evergreen leaves. Half shade or shade.

Hosta (funkia)

A perennial which comes into leaf in the spring. Flowers appear on tall stems in the summer but flower arrangers grow the hosta for its wonderful foliage. There are many different varieties of different sizes with different variegations. Shade.

Tellima

Round evergreen leaves which grow close to the ground. Long delicate green-yellow bell-shaped flowers from April to June. A good source of strong leaves throughout the winter. Half shade or shade.

Virginia creeper

Deciduous self-supporting climber, ideal for walls, with glossy leaves which are a vibrant green until the autumn when they change to glorious reds, yellows and oranges. The leaves are some of the last to fall. The partly three-lobed species are generally more useful than those with leaves divided into leaflets.

Fillers

Alchemilla mollis (lady's mantle)

One of the best of fillers, sadly only available about four months of the year from June to September. Sprays of lime-green flowers which add something to every arrangement. Although it will grow in the sun it needs a moist soil. The leaves are good concealers.

Choisya ternata (Mexican orange)

An extremely easy shrub to grow, it spreads quickly once established. It has divided leaves which are glossy and evergreen and aromatic white flowers throughout the spring and summer. The fragrance is not to everyone's taste. Sun or partial shade.

Conifer

In wintertime little can take the place of conifer. It lasts well and is evocative of the Christmas season. It can also be used as line.

Euonymus

There are many varieties of euonymus and they are all useful. They are mainly evergreen. Two particularly useful varieties are *Euonymus japonicus* 'Aureo-pictus' with a bright yellow splash in the centre of each leaf which brightens up the winter garden or north-facing garden and the *Euonymus fortunei* which will climb up a wall.

Euphorbla (spurge)

Lots of varieties but the conspicuous bracts of the evergreen varieties give interest in the garden for many months of the year. Spreads rapidly. Excellent in tubs as it tolerates erratic watering.

Hebe (veronica)

Compact evergreen shrub. Many varieties are hardy and easy-going. They grow easily from cuttings and flower profusely in a sunny site. Those with small neat leaves are generally more useful to the flower arranger.

Laurel

Laurel together with its relative 'Spotted Laurel' fills in many a pedestal arrangement. It is extremely easy to grow.

Also see ceanothus, pittosporum, *Viburnum tinus*, skimmia.

Senecio

A good-natured grey-leaved plant with bright yellow flowers during July and August. Sun or light shade.

Variegated holly

Plant this shrub first as it does grow slowly. It is a most beautiful shrub, especially in winter. Sprays from the golden variegated 'Golden Queen' are magical in Christmas arrangements. Unfortunately it does not bear berries.

Focal material

As mentioned in chapter 1, focal material tends to be flowers rather than foliage.

Achillea

A hardy perennial with flat flower heads. The yellow and golden variet-ies are particularly useful to the flower arranger as they dry well and retain good colour. The entire flowering stems are excellent in large arrangements and snippets can be taken from the main flower head to add to miniature arrangements.

Chrysanthemums

Hardy chrysanthemums are free-flowering mostly during the late summer and autumn months. There is a vast range of types and colours. Removing the growing tip in June encourages bushy side growths and increased flowering.

Dahlias

Dahlias do not grow from a bulb but from a tuber which should be lifted and stored during the winter months. This is not always easy, but they are worth the effort because they give a troublefree display of bright flowers from late summer until the heavy frosts. Sun.

Hellebores (Christmas rose, Lenten rose)

Evergreen plants which flower in winter. They last extremely well once cut if the stamens are allowed to disappear and the seeds form in the centre of the flower. Otherwise boiling, burning, scoring or immersing in water does little to stop them drooping. They are enchanting when added to any arrangement. Shade.

Hydrangea

Hydrangeas can be grown on any soil but on lime soil the blue varieties will turn pink or purple-red and on acid soil the pink varieties may turn blue or purple-blue. The hortensia group is best for flower arranging generally as they dry much better than the lacecaps. Excellent in large arrangements where bulk and strong form is needed. When planted they need to be well watered in. Sun or shade.

Peony

Such handsome flowers. All varieties are wonderful and easy to grow once established. When they are established try not to move them. They hang dry extremely easily. When using the foliage do not remove the bottom leaves from the stems as the flower is not as likely to develop. Their foliage is good and long-lasting.

Poppies

Short-lived flowers in a stunning array of colours. So easy to grow – just throw the seeds onto the ground in March or April. The seedheads are invaluable in dried flower arrangements. Sun or partial shade.

Roses

All roses are lovely in arrangements. Sun or shade.

Rudbeckia

Bright yellow flowers on firm stems July to October. Easy to grow in well-drained sunny site.

Sedum

The tiny flowers grow in dense groups and form a flattened head. *Sedum spectabile* 'Autumn Joy' is thought by many flower arrangers to be one of the best. It dries extremely well in situ and is easy to use in dried flower arrangements. Most varieties like well-drained soil in full sun and survive well in the most severe of droughts. Bees love sedum.

────── APPENDIX 3 ──────

────────── Houseplants ──────────

Line material

Boston fern, hart's-tongue fern (*Nephrolepis exaltata, Phyllitis scolopendrium*)

These and many others are extremely useful. They are quick and easy to grow. They do need a moist atmosphere. The Boston fern is ideal for a hanging basket, where it will give a wonderful fountain of greenery.

Cast iron plant (aspidistra)

Line or concealer in large arrangements. Easy to grow, it can be planted outside in very sheltered areas. The only disadvantage is that it takes so long to grow. Leaves can be curved round to give enclosed space (as you can with tulip leaves).

Mother-in-law's tongue, snake plant (sansevieria)

Easy to insert on a pinholder. Once inserted in foam it lasts well. Easy-going.

Parlour palm (*Neathe bella*)

For very large arrangements, it conditions well and is long-lasting and easy-going.

Silk oak, Australian wattle (*Grevillea robusta*)

Line or filler plant material with beautiful silvery foliage. Do not allow to dry out. Conditions well and is long-lasting.

Wandering jew (*Tradescantia albiflora*)

Green and white trailing line material. Easy to propagate.

Weeping fig, willow fig (*Ficus benjamina*)

Line or filler. Lasts well and is easy to insert in foam.

Filler material

Aluminium plant, friendship plant (pilea)

Easy to grow but dislikes strong sunshine. Very decorative.

Asparagus fern, maidenhair ferns (*Asparagus plumosus* and *Adiantum cuneatum*)

Easy to grow and long-lasting, they are beautiful foils to any flowers.

Dragon plant (dracaena)

Thin wiry stems, long-lasting.

Flame nettle (coleus)

Wonderful colours in different varieties but not always easy to grow.

Grape ivy (*Cissus rhombifolia*)

Exceptionally easy-going and quick to grow.

Spider plant (chlorophytum)

Sprays of spider plant can be added as filler to any arrangement. Exceptionally good-natured plant. One of the easiest to grow. Individual leaves can be used as line but are rather floppy.

Concealer material

Begonia rex

Triangular leaves ranging in colour from silver to pink to purple. They have wonderful texture. Easy to insert in foam and lasts well if conditioned.

Cape grape

Extremely easy to grow and tolerant of most conditions.

Crotons (Codiaeum variegatum pictum)

Patterned red, orange, yellow, green and black. Needs warm dry atmosphere away from direct sunshine. Loses lower leaves when mature.

Devil's ivy (Scindapsus aureus)

Heart-shaped green and yellow leaves. Best in slight shade. Easy to grow and lasts in foam.

Goose foot plant (Syngonium podophyllum)

Easy-going arrow-headed plant which lasts well. Lovely light green colouring.

Persina violet (cyclamen)

Easy to insert in foam and lasts well. Dislikes dry conditions but crown must not be wetted, so water from underneath.

Rose of China, Chinese rose (hibiscus)

Easy to grow and use.

Also see fatsia, fatshedera, ivy, tolmeia, geranium.

Rubber plant (*Ficus elastica*)

Excellent long-lasting shiny leaves on rigid stem. It loses its leaves as it matures but these can be used in arrangements.

Spotted laurel (acuba)

Conditions well and is long-lasting. Easy to grow. For larger designs use sprays.

Swiss cheese plant (*Monstera deliciosa*)

Enormous glossy long-lasting leaves. Startlingly effective in large arrangements.

Focal material

Chrysanthemums

Excellent for flower arranging. They are sturdy, tolerant of centrally heated homes and come in a wide variety of colours.

Also see hydrangea and geranium.

Roses

These grow easily in containers. They will flower earlier in the home. Varieties of hybrid tea roses grown for the florist trade are excellent, as are the 'Garnette' roses which are long-lasting on and off the plant.

—— APPENDIX 4 ——

—————— Wild plant material ——————

The following is a selection of wild plant material widely available in many parts of the country. It is of course essential to observe the Country Code when out foraging for your material. This means that you should only take material from where it grows in abundance and even then pick in moderation. Never uproot any plant. There are many seeds on sale for growing wild flowers such as primroses in your garden. If you are in any doubt as to the rarity of a flower do not pick without first checking in a reference book.

The wild plant material listed below has been roughly divided into seasons. In many cases the seasons overlap.

Spring

Birch

Hedgerows, motorway verges. Extremely pliant line material.

Catkins, pussy willow, wild arum, hart's-tongue fern

See *winter*.

Cow parsley

Hedge banks, riverbanks, motorway verges. White flowers superb as filler. Late spring.

Daisy

Lawns, pastures, hedgerows. Flowers pink and white. Point in miniature. Flowers press well.

Herb Robert

Shady walls, stony places. Leaves excellent for pressing.

Ivy

Found on trees and in hedgerows. Sprays of line material and concealer leaves.

Jack-by-the-hedge (garlic mustard, sauce alone)

Waste ground, shady banks. Coarse leafy plant. White filler flowers.

Lady's smock (cuckoo flower)

Dampish places. Lilac flowers late spring.

Lesser celandine

Woods and hedgerows. Bright yellow flowers. Flowers close in the cold and open in the sun.

Privet

Hedgerows and thickets. Line and filler material.

Ragwort

Wasteland and pastures. Tough weed with showy yellow filler flowers. Late spring.

Red dead nettle

Garden and field weed. Leaves are excellent for pressing. Flowers as filler.

Summer

Beech

Woodland. Line and filler. In July preserve leaves in glycerine solution.

Bird's-foot trefoil

Pastures and heaths. Orange-yellow dainty flowers for small arrangements.

Cow parsley

Summer seedheads can be picked for drying. They must not be too ripe.

Dog rose

Hedgerows. Delicate focal flowers. Sprays give line material.

Feverfew (mayweed)

Fields, sea-cliffs. Mini daisy-like 'focal' flowers. Use as filler.

Grasses

Everywhere. Line material, many varieties. Pick in June for drying. Place flat on paper.

Hogsweed

Meadows and waste ground. Hogsweed is extremely poisonous. Wash hands after handling. A bold flower head. Use alone in a vase.

Honeysuckle

Hedges and thickets. Also known as woodbine. Flowers are cream tinged with yellow and red. Sprays of curved line material.

Oak

Woodland. Line and filler. In July preserve leaves in glycerine solution (see page 98).

Ox-eye daisy (moon daisy)

Meadows, motorway verges. White 'focal' flowers. Also use as filler.

Rosebay willow herb (fireweed)

Wasteland and open woodland. Showy filler for large arrangements. Flowers rosy purple late summer.

Sorrel

Fields, verges. Crimson and green line flowers. Pick and dry upside down before too mature for dried arrangements.

Autumn

Bracken

Moor, heaths, hedgerows. Filler, concealer for large arrangements. Pick before completely brown and press under a carpet between newspaper.

Bramble

Hedges and thickets. Purple or black fruits on graceful sprays for line material. Shorter pieces can be used as filler.

Clematis (old man's beard)

Hedges and thickets. It is more abundant on chalk. Long feathery line material. A spray of hair lacquer will stop the seeds from floating off.

Dock

Waste land. Green line flowers tinged red. Flowers in small whorls. Dry upside down before too mature for dried arrangements.

Dog rose

Hedgerows. Long-lasting scarlet hips. Lovely in all arrangements.

Ferns

Shady banks. Different varieties in different parts of the country. Line and concealer. Some ferns are rare so do not pick if in doubt.

Heather

Heathland, moorland. Pink and purple flowers. Line for small designs, filler for larger. Can be hung upside down in small groups to dry.

Privet

Hedgerows, thickets. Small black berries which are long-lasting. Strip off the leaves to show off the fruits.

Ragwort

Roadsides, agricultural land. A troublesome weed. Showy bright yellow filler flowers.

St John's wort

Meadows and dry places. Smallish yellow point flowers. Wonderful long-lasting fruits.

Teasels

Waste land. Flowers pale purple on stiff stems. Point and filler.

Yarrow

Roadsides, fields. Flowers from June but later blooms last longest when cut.

Winter

Beech

Woodland. Woody brown nuts on sturdy stalks. Lovely texture and form.

Broom

Roadsides, heaths, moor. Good line material.

Conifer

Woodland. Cones invaluable at Christmas time.

Dog's mercury

Woods and shady banks. Filler. The inconspicuous flowers are excellent pressed. February onwards.

Hart's-tongue fern

Hedgerows, shady banks. Sturdy line material throughout the year.

Hazel catkins

Hedgerows and woodland. January to March. Excellent for landscapes or mixed in vases with bulb flowers.

Holly

Hedgerows, woodland. Long-lasting filler or line material for Christmas. Leave the berries for the birds and add artificial ones at home.

Ivy

Trees and hedgerows. Line concealer leaves. Fruits give wonderful form and texture. Can be sprayed gold for Christmas.

Larch

Woodland. Sprays with cones provide line material, good for landscape designs and mixed with bulb flowers in a vase.

Pussy willow

Hedgerow, woodland. Line material, landscapes, mixed with bulb flowers.

Wild arum (lords and ladies, cuckoo pint)

Woods, shady banks. Leaves wonderful in landscapes. Excellent at base of elongated triangle. Concealer leaves for medium to large designs.

INDEX